BRITISH R  **.3**

MULTIPLE S

SEVENTEENTH EDITION
2004

The complete guide to all Diesel Multiple
Units which operate on National Rail

Peter Fox & Robert Pritchard

UPDATED TO 2005 EDITION 1·1·05

ISBN 1 902336 34 8

Pocket

CONTENTS

PROVISION OF INFORMATION

This book has been compiled with care to be as accurate as possible, but in some cases official information is not available and the publisher cannot be held responsible for any errors or omissions. We would like to thank the companies and individuals which have been co-operative in supplying information to us. The authors of this series of books will be pleased to receive notification from readers of any inaccuracies readers may find in the series, and notification of any additional information to supplement our records and thus enhance future editions is always welcome. Please send comments to:

Robert Pritchard, Platform 5 Publishing Ltd., Wyvern House, Sark Road, Sheffield, S2 4HG, England.
Tel: 0114 255 2625 **Fax:** 0114 255 2471
e-mail: robert@platform5.com

Both the author and the staff of Platform 5 regret they are unable to answer specific queries regarding locomotives and rolling stock.

This book is updated to 17 November 2003.

UPDATES

An update to all the books in the *British Railways Pocket Book* series is published every month in the Platform 5 magazine, entra, which contains news and rolling stock information on the railways of Britain and Ireland. For further details of entra please see the advertisement on the back cover of this book.

BRITAIN'S RAILWAY SYSTEM

INFRASTRUCTURE & OPERATION

Britain's national railway infrastructure is now owned by a "not for dividend" company, Network Rail, following the demise of Railtrack. Many stations and maintenance depots are leased to and operated by Train Operating Companies (TOCs), but some larger stations remain under Network Rail control. The only exception is the infrastructure on the Isle of Wight, which is nationally owned and is leased to the Island Line franchisee.

Trains are operated by TOCs over Network Rail, regulated by access agreements between the parties involved. In general, TOCs are responsible for the provision and maintenance of the locomotives, rolling stock and staff necessary for the direct operation of services, whilst Network Rail is responsible for the provision and maintenance of the infrastructure and also for staff needed to regulate the operation of services.

DOMESTIC PASSENGER TRAIN OPERATORS

The large majority of passenger trains are operated by the TOCs on fixed term franchises. Franchise expiry dates are shown in parentheses in the list of franchisees below:

Franchise	Franchisee	Trading Name
Anglia Railways[2]	GB Railways plc. (until 4 April 2004)	Anglia Railways
Central Trains	National Express Group plc (until 1 April 2006)	Central Trains
Chiltern Railways	M40 Trains Ltd. (until December 2021)	Chiltern Railways
Cross-Country[1]	Virgin Rail Group Ltd. (until March 2012)	Virgin Trains
Gatwick Express	National Express Group plc (until 27 April 2011)	Gatwick Express
Great Eastern Railway[2]	First Group plc (until 4 April 2004)	First Great Eastern
Great Western Trains	First Group plc (until 3 February 2006)	First Great Western
InterCity East Coast	GNER Holdings Ltd. (until 4 April 2005)	Great North Eastern Railway
InterCity West Coast[1]	Virgin Rail Group Ltd. (until 8 March 2012)	Virgin Trains
Island Line	Stagecoach Holdings plc (until February 2007)	Island Line
LTS Rail	National Express Group plc (until 25 May 2011)	c2c
Merseyrail Electrics[3]	Serco/NedRail (until 20 July 2028)	Merseyrail Electrics

Midland Main Line	National Express Group plc (until 27 April 2008)	Midland Mainline
North London Railways	National Express Group plc (until 1 September 2006)	Silverlink Train Services
North West Regional Railways[4]	First Group plc (until 1 April 2004)	First North Western
Regional Railways North East[4]	Arriva Trains Ltd	Arriva Trains Northern
ScotRail	National Express Group plc (until 30 September 2004)	ScotRail
South Central	GoVia Ltd. (Go-Ahead/Keolis). (until May 2010)	South Central
South Eastern[5]		South Eastern Trains
South West	Stagecoach Holdings plc (until 3 February 2007)	South West Trains
Thames[6]	Go-Ahead Group (until 31 March 2004)	Thames Trains
Thameslink	GoVia Ltd. (until 1 April 2006)	Thameslink Rail
Wales & Borders[7]	National Express Group plc (until 6 December 2003)	Wales & Borders Trains
Wessex Trains	National Express Group plc (until 30 April 2006)	Wessex Trains
West Anglia Great Northern[8]	National Express Group plc (until 4 April 2004)	WAGN

Notes:

[1] Franchise to be renegotiated by April 2004.

[2] Due to transfer to new Greater Anglia franchise, expected to be formed in April 2004.

[3] Now under control of Merseyrail PTE instead of the Strategic Rail Authority (SRA). Franchise due to be reviewed after seven years and then every five years to fit in with Merseyside Local Transport Plan.

[4] Urban and rural services currently run by Arriva Trains Northern and First North Western are due to transfer to the new Northern franchise in late 2004. Trans-Pennine services run by these operators will be taken over by the new Trans-Pennine Express franchise on 1 February 2004.

[5] New interim management company known as South Eastern Trains (SET) formed on 9 November 2003, pending award of new Integrated Kent franchise expected in early 2005. SET is a subsidiary of the SRA.

[6] Due to transfer to First Group on 1 April 2004 for two years.

[7] Arriva Trains Ltd due to take over from National Express Group on 7 December 2003 for 15 years.

[8] West Anglia half of WAGN due to transfer to new Greater Anglia franchise. A number of options are being considered for Great Northern services, including transfer to another franchise.

A major reorganisation of franchises is under way. See **entrain** for developments.

The following operators run non-franchised services only:

Operator	Trading Name	Route
British Airports Authority	Heathrow Express	London Paddington–Heathrow Airport
Hull Trains	Hull Trains	London King's Cross–Hull
West Coast Railway Co.	West Coast Railway	Fort William–Mallaig*
		York–Scarborough*

* Special summer-dated services only.

INTERNATIONAL PASSENGER OPERATIONS

Eurostar (UK) operates international passenger-only services between the United Kingdom and continental Europe, jointly with French National Railways (SNCF) and Belgian National Railways (SNCB/NMBS). Eurostar (UK) is a subsidiary of London & Continental Railways, which is jointly owned by National Express Group plc and British Airways.

In addition, a service for the conveyance of accompanied road vehicles through the Channel Tunnel is provided by the tunnel operating company, Eurotunnel.

FREIGHT TRAIN OPERATIONS

The following operators operate freight train services under 'Open Access' arrangements:

English Welsh & Scottish Railway Ltd (EWS).
Freightliner Ltd.
GB Railfreight Ltd. (now owned by First Group)
Direct Rail Services Ltd.

INTRODUCTION

DMU CLASSES

DMU Classes are listed in class number order. Principal details and dimensions are quoted for each class in metric and/or imperial units as considered appropriate bearing in mind common usage in the UK.

All dimensions and weights are quoted for vehicles in an "as new" condition with all necessary supplies (e.g. oil, water, sand) on board. Dimensions are quoted in the order Length – Width. All lengths quoted are over buffers or couplers as appropriate. All width dimensions quoted are maxima.

NUMERICAL LISTINGS

DMUs are listed in numerical order of set – using current numbers as allocated by the RSL. Individual 'loose' vehicles are listed in numerical order after vehicles formed into fixed formations. Where numbers carried are different from those officially allocated these are noted in class headings where appropriate. Where sets or vehicles have been renumbered in recent years, former numbering detail is shown in parentheses. Each entry is laid out as in the following example:

Set No.	Detail	Livery	Owner	Operation	Depot	Formation
170 636	r	**CT**	P	*CT*	TS	50636 56636 79636

Detail Differences. Detail differences which currently affect the areas and types of train which vehicles may work are shown, plus differences in interior layout. Where such differences occur within a class, these are shown either in the heading information or alongside the individual set or vehicle number. The following standard abbreviation is used:

r   Radio Electronic Token Block (RETB) equipment.

In all cases use of the above abbreviations indicates the equipment indicated is normally operable. Meaning of non-standard abbreviations is detailed in individual class headings.

Set Formations. Regular set formations are shown where these are normally maintained. Readers should note set formations might be temporarily varied from time to time to suit maintenance and/or operational requirements. Vehicles shown as "spare" are not formed in any regular set formation.

Codes. Codes are used to denote the livery, owner, operation and depot of each unit. Details of these will be found in section 5 of this book. Where a unit or spare car is off-lease, the operation column will be left blank.

Names. Only names carried with official sanction are listed. As far as possible names are shown in UPPER/lower case characters as actually shown on the name carried on the vehicle(s). Unless otherwise shown, complete units are regarded as named rather than just the individual car(s) which carry the name.

GENERAL INFORMATION

CLASSIFICATION AND NUMBERING

First generation ("Heritage") DMUs are classified in the series 100–139.
Second generation DMUs are classified in the series 140–199.
Diesel-electric multiple units are classified in the series 200–249.
Service units are classified in the series 930–999.
First and second generation individual cars are numbered in the series 50000–59999 and 79000–79999.

DEMU individual cars are numbered in the series 60000–60999, except for a few former EMU vehicles which retain their EMU numbers.

Service stock individual cars are numbered in the series 975000–975999 and 977000–977999, although this series is not exclusively used for DMU vehicles.

OPERATING CODES

These codes are used by train operating company staff to describe the various different types of vehicles and normally appear on data panels on the inner (i.e. non driving) ends of vehicles.

The first part of the code describes whether or not the car has a motor or a driving cab as follows:

DM Driving motor.
M   Motor
DT   Driving trailer
T   Trailer

The next letter is a "B" for cars with a brake compartment.

This is followed by the saloon details:

F   First
S   Standard
C   Composite
so denotes a semi-open vehicle (part compartments, part open). All other vehicles are assumed to consist solely of open saloons.

L denotes a vehicle with a lavatory compartment.

Finally vehicles with a buffet are suffixed RB or RMB for a miniature buffet.

Where two vehicles of the same type are formed within the same unit, the above codes may be suffixed by (A) and (B) to differentiate between the vehicles.

A composite is a vehicle containing both first and standard class accommodation, whilst a brake vehicle is a vehicle containing separate specific accommodation for the conductor.

Special Note: Where vehicles have been declassified, the correct operating code which describes the actual vehicle layout is quoted in this publication.

BUILD DETAILS

Lot Numbers

Vehicles ordered under the auspices of BR were allocated a Lot (batch) number when ordered and these are quoted in class headings and sub-headings. Vehicles ordered since 1995 have no Lot Numbers, but the manufacturer and location that they were built is given.

ACCOMMODATION

The information given in class headings and sub-headings is in the form F/S nT (or TD) nW. For example 12/54 1T 1W denotes 12 first class and 54 standard class seats, one toilet and one space for a wheelchair. The seating layout of open saloons is shown as 2+1, 2+2 or 3+2 as the case may be. Where units have first class accommodation as well as standard and the layout is different for each class then these are shown separately prefixed by "1:" and "2:". Compartments are always three seats a side in first class and four a side in standard class in DMUs. TD denotes a toilet suitable for a disabled person.

ABBREVIATIONS

The following abbreviations are used in class headings and also throughout this publication:

BR	British Railways.
BSI	Bergische Stahl Industrie.
DEMU	Diesel electric multiple unit.
DMU	Diesel multiple unit (general term).
EMU	Electric multiple unit.
kN	kilonewtons.
km/h	kilometres per hour.
kW	kilowatts.
LT	London Transport.
LUL	London Underground Limited.
m.	metres.
m.p.h.	miles per hour.
t.	tonnes.

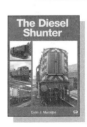

1. DIESEL MECHANICAL & DIESEL HYDRAULIC UNITS

1.1 FIRST GENERATION UNITS

CLASS 101   METRO-CAMMELL

First generation units still in service with First North Western. Due for withdrawal by the end of 2003. DMBS–DMSL.

Construction: Aluminium alloy body on steel underframe.
Engines: Two Leyland 680/1 of 112 kW (150 h.p.) at 1800 r.p.m. per power car.
Transmission: Mechanical. Cardan shaft and freewheel to a four-speed epicyclic gearbox with a further cardan shaft to the final drive, each engine driving the inner axle of one bogie.
Brakes: Vacuum.
Gangways: British Standard (Midland scissors type). Within unit only.
Bogies: DD15 (motor) and DT11 (trailer).
Couplers: Screw couplings.
Dimensions: 18.49 x 2.82 m.
Seating Layout: 3+2 mainly unidirectional.
Doors: Manually-operated slam.
Multiple Working: 'Blue Square' coupling code. First generation vehicles may be coupled together to work in multiple up to a maximum of 6 motor cars or 12 cars in total in a formation. First generation vehicles may not be coupled in multiple with second generation vehicles.
Maximum Speed: 70 m.p.h.

51192/51205/51210. DMBS. Lot No. 30467 1958–1959. –/52. 32.5 t.
53164. DMBS. Lot No. 30546 1956. –/52. 32.5 t.
53204. DMBS. Lot No. 30259 1957. –/52. 32.5 t.
53253. DMBS. Lot No. 30266 1957. –/52. 32.5 t.
51511. DMSL. Lot No. 30501 1959. –/58. 32.5 t.
51803. DMSL. Lot No. 30588 1959. –/72 1T. 32.5 t.
53160. DMSL. Lot No. 30253 1956. –/72 1T. 32.5 t.
53170. DMSL. Lot No. 30255 1957. –/72 1T. 32.5 t.
53266. DMSL. Lot No. 30267 1957. –/72 1T. 32.5 t.
53746. DMSL. Lot No. 30271 1957. –/72 1T. 32.5 t.

Non-standard livery: 101 692 is in Caledonian style blue with yellow/orange stripes.

101 676	RR	A	NW	LO	51205	51803
101 678	RR	A	NW	LO	51210	53746
101 680	RR	A	NW	LO	53204	51511
101 685	G	A	NW	LO	53164	53160
101 692	O	A		LO	53253	53170
101 693	S	A	NW	LO	51192	53266

CLASS 121   PRESSED STEEL SUBURBAN

First generation unit used by Chiltern Railways on selected Aylesbury– Princes Risborough services.
Construction: Steel.
Engines: Two Leyland 1595 of 112 kW (150 h.p.) at 1800 r.p.m.
Transmission: Mechanical. Cardan shaft and freewheel to a four-speed epicyclic gearbox and final drive.
Brakes: Vacuum.   **Couplers:** Screw couplings.
Gangways: Non gangwayed single cars with cabs at each end.
Bogies: DD10.   **Seating Layout:** 3+2 facing.
Dimensions: 20.45 x 2.82 m.   **Maximum Speed:** 70 m.p.h.
Doors: Manually-operated slam.   **Multiple Working:** As Class 101.

55020. DMBS. Lot No. 30518 1960. –/65. 38.0 t.

Non-standard livery: 121 020 is all over Chiltern blue with a silver stripe.

Note: Also fitted with Central Door Locking.

121 020   **0**   CR   *CR*   AL   55020

1.2 SECOND GENERATION UNITS

All units in this section have air brakes and are equipped with public address, with transmission equipment on driving vehicles and flexible diaphragm gangways. Except where otherwise stated, transmission is Voith 211r hydraulic with a cardan shaft to a Gmeinder GM190 final drive.

CLASS 142   PACER   BREL DERBY/LEYLAND

DMS–DMSL.

Construction: Steel. Built from Leyland National bus parts on four-wheeled underframes.
Engines: One Cummins LTA10-R of 172 kW (230 h.p.) at 2100 r.p.m.
(* One Perkins 2006-TWH of 172 kW (230 h.p.) at 2100 r.p.m.).
Couplers: BSI at outer ends, bar within unit.
Seating Layout: 3+2 mainly unidirectional bus/bench style unless stated.
Dimensions: 15.66 x 2.80 m.
Gangways: Within unit only.   **Wheel Arrangement:** 1-A A-1.
Doors: Twin-leaf inward pivoting. **Maximum Speed:** 75 m.p.h.
Multiple Working: Within class and with Classes 143, 144, 150, 153, 155, 156, 158, 159.

55542–55591. DMS. Lot No. 31003 1985–1986. –/62 (s –/56, t –/53 or 55 1W, u –/52 or 54 1W, v –/52 1W) 23.26 t.
55592–55641. DMSL. Lot No. 31004 1985–1986. –/59 1T (s –/50 1T, u –/60 1T, v –/50 1T) 24.97 t.
55701–55746. DMS. Lot No. 31013 1986–1987. –/62 (s –/56, t –/53 or 55 1W, u –/52 or 54 1W, v–/52 1W) 23.26 t.
55747–55792. DMSL. Lot No. 31014 1986–1987. –/59 1T (s –/50 1T, u –/60 1T, v–/50 1T) 24.97 t.

s Fitted with 2+2 individual high-backed seating.
t First North Western facelifted units – DMS fitted with luggage rack and wheelchair space.
u Merseytravel units – Fitted with 3+2 individual low-back seating.
v Refurbished Valley Lines units. Fitted with 2+2 individual Chapman seating.

142 001	t	**NW**	A	*NW*	NH	55542	55592
142 002	v	**VL**	A	*VL*	CF	55543	55593
142 003	t	**NW**	A	*NW*	NH	55544	55594
142 004	t	**NW**	A	*NW*	NH	55545	55595
142 005	t	**NW**	A	*NW*	NH	55546	55596
142 006	v	**VL**	A	*VL*	CF	55547	55597
142 007	t	**NW**	A	*NW*	NH	55548	55598
142 009	t	**NW**	A	*NW*	NH	55550	55600

Newton Heath 125
1876–2001

142 010	v	**VL**	A	*VL*	CF	55551	55601
142 011	t	**NW**	A	*NW*	NH	55552	55602
142 012	t	**NW**	A	*NW*	NH	55553	55603
142 013	t	**NW**	A	*NW*	NH	55554	55604
142 014	t	**NW**	A	*NW*	NH	55555	55605
142 015	s	**RR**	A	*AN*	HT	55556	55606
142 016	s	**RR**	A	*AN*	HT	55557	55607
142 017	s	**AV**	A	*AN*	HT	55558	55608
142 018	s	**AV**	A	*AN*	HT	55559	55609
142 019	s	**TW**	A	*AN*	HT	55560	55610
142 020	s	**AV**	A	*AN*	HT	55561	55611
142 021	s	**AV**	A	*AN*	HT	55562	55612
142 022	s	**TW**	A	*AN*	HT	55563	55613
142 023	t	**NW**	A	*NW*	NH	55564	55614
142 024	s	**RR**	A	*AN*	HT	55565	55615
142 025	s	**NS**	A	*AN*	HT	55566	55616
142 026	s	**NS**	A	*AN*	HT	55567	55617
142 027	t	**NW**	A	*NW*	NH	55568	55618
142 028	t	**NW**	A	*NW*	NH	55569	55619
142 029	t	**NW**	A	*NW*	NH	55570	55620
142 030	t	**NW**	A	*NW*	NH	55571	55621
142 031	t	**NW**	A	*NW*	NH	55572	55622
142 032	t	**NW**	A	*NW*	NH	55573	55623
142 033	t	**NW**	A	*NW*	NH	55574	55624
142 034	t	**NW**	A	*NW*	NH	55575	55625
142 035	t	**NW**	A	*NW*	NH	55576	55626
142 036	t	**NW**	A	*NW*	NH	55577	55627
142 037	t	**NW**	A	*NW*	NH	55578	55628
142 038	t	**NW**	A	*NW*	NH	55579	55629
142 039	t	**NW**	A	*NW*	NH	55580	55630
142 040	t	**NW**	A	*NW*	NH	55581	55631
142 041	u	**MY**	A	*NW*	NH	55582	55632
142 042	u	**MY**	A	*NW*	NH	55583	55633
142 043	u	**MY**	A	*NW*	NH	55584	55634
142 044	u	**MY**	A	*NW*	NH	55585	55635
142 045	u	**MY**	A	*NW*	NH	55586	55636

142 046	u	MY	A	NW	NH	55587	55637	
142 047	u	MY	A	NW	NH	55588	55638	
142 048	u	MY	A	NW	NH	55589	55639	
142 049	u	MY	A	NW	NH	55590	55640	
142 050	s	NS	A	AN	HT	55591	55641	
142 051	u	MY	A	NW	NH	55701	55747	
142 052	u	MY	A	NW	NH	55702	55748	
142 053	u	MY	A	NW	NH	55703	55749	
142 054	u	MT	A	NW	NH	55704	55750	
142 055	u	MY	A	NW	NH	55705	55751	
142 056	u	MY	A	NW	NH	55706	55752	
142 057	u	MT	A	NW	NH	55707	55753	
142 058	u	MT	A	NW	NH	55708	55754	
142 060	t	NW	A	NW	NH	55710	55756	
142 061	t	NW	A	NW	NH	55711	55757	
142 062	t	NW	A	NW	NH	55712	55758	
142 063	t	NW	A	NW	NH	55713	55759	
142 064	t	NW	A	NW	NH	55714	55760	
142 065	s	NS	A	AN	HT	55715	55761	
142 066	s	NS	A	AN	HT	55716	55762	
142 067	t	NW	A	NW	NH	55717	55763	
142 068	t	NW	A	NW	NH	55718	55764	
142 069	v	VL	A	VL	CF	55719	55765	
142 070	t	NW	A	NW	NH	55720	55766	
142 071	s	RR	A	AN	HT	55721	55767	
142 072	v	VL	A	VL	CF	55722	55768	
142 073	v	VL	A	VL	CF	55723	55769	Myfanwy
142 074	v	VL	A	VL	CF	55724	55770	
142 075	v	VL	A	VL	CF	55725	55771	
142 076	v	VL	A	VL	CF	55726	55772	
142 077	v	VL	A	VL	CF	55727	55773	
142 078	s	RR	A	AN	HT	55728	55774	
142 079	s	RR	A	AN	HT	55729	55775	
142 080	v	VL	A	VL	CF	55730	55776	Caerphilly R. F. C.
142 081	v	VW	A	VL	CF	55731	55777	
142 082	v	VL	A	VL	CF	55732	55778	
142 083	v	VL	A	VL	CF	55733	55779	
142 084	s*	RR	A	AN	HT	55734	55780	
142 085	v	VL	A	VL	CF	55735	55781	
142 086	s	RR	A	AN	HT	55736	55782	
142 087	s	RR	A	AN	HT	55737	55783	
142 088	s	RR	A	AN	HT	55738	55784	
142 089	s	RR	A	AN	HT	55739	55785	
142 090	s	RR	A	AN	HT	55740	55786	
142 091	s	RR	A	AN	HT	55741	55787	
142 092	s	RR	A	AN	HT	55742	55788	
142 093	s	RR	A	AN	HT	55743	55789	
142 094	s	RR	A	AN	HT	55744	55790	
142 095	s	RR	A	AN	HT	55745	55791	
142 096	s	RR	A	AN	HT	55746	55792	

CLASS 143   PACER   ALEXANDER/BARCLAY

DMS–DMSL. Similar design to Class 142, but bodies built by W. Alexander with Barclay underframes.

Construction: Steel. Alexander bus bodywork on four-wheeled underframes.
Engines: One Cummins LTA10-R of 172 kW (230 h.p.) at 2100 r.p.m.
Couplers: BSI at outer ends, bar couplers within unit.
Seating Layout: All units are now fitted with 2+2 high-back Chapman seating, mainly unidirectional.
Dimensions: 15.55 x 2.70 m.
Gangways: Within unit only.   **Wheel Arrangement:** 1-A A-1.
Doors: Twin-leaf inward pivoting.   **Maximum Speed:** 75 m.p.h.
Multiple Working: Within class and with Classes 142, 144, 150, 153, 155, 156, 158, 159.

DMS. Lot No. 31005 Andrew Barclay 1985–1986. –/55. 24.5 t.
DMSL. Lot No. 31006 Andrew Barclay 1985–1986. –/51 1T. 25.0 t.

143 601	VL	RD	VL	CF	55642	55667	
143 602	VL	P	VL	CF	55651	55668	
143 603	BI	P	WX	CF	55658	55669	
143 604	VL	P	VL	CF	55645	55670	
143 605	VL	P	VL	CF	55646	55671	Crimestoppers
143 606	VL	P	VL	CF	55647	55672	
143 607	VL	P	VL	CF	55648	55673	
143 608	VL	P	VL	CF	55649	55674	
143 609	VL	BC	VL	CF	55650	55675	Tom Jones
143 610	VL	RD	VL	CF	55643	55676	
143 611	BI	P	WX	CF	55652	55677	
143 612	BI	P	WX	CF	55653	55678	
143 613	BI	P	WX	CF	55654	55679	
143 614	VL	RD	VL	CF	55655	55680	
143 615	VL	P	VL	CF	55656	55681	
143 616	VL	P	VL	CF	55657	55682	
143 617	BI	RI	WX	CF	55644	55683	
143 618	BI	RI	WX	CF	55659	55684	
143 619	BI	RI	WX	CF	55660	55685	
143 620	BI	P	WX	CF	55661	55686	
143 621	BI	P	VL	CF	55662	55687	
143 622	BI	P	VL	CF	55663	55688	
143 623	BI	P	WX	CF	55664	55689	
143 624	VL	P	VL	CF	55665	55690	
143 625	VL	P	VL	CF	55666	55691	Valley Kids

CLASS 144 PACER ALEXANDER/BREL DERBY

DMS–DMSL or DMS–MS–DMSL. As Class 143, but underframes built by BREL.

Construction: Steel. Alexander bus bodywork on four-wheeled underframes.
Engines: One Cummins LTA10-R of 172 kW (230 h.p.) at 2100 r.p.m.
Couplers: BSI at outer ends, bar couplers within unit.
Seating Layout: 3+2 mainly unidirectional bus/bench style unless stated.
Dimensions: 15.55 x 2.73 m.
Gangways: Within unit only.   **Wheel Arrangement:** 1-A A-1.
Doors: Twin-leaf inward pivoting.   **Maximum Speed:** 75 m.p.h.
Multiple Working: Within class and with Classes 142, 143, 150, 153, 155, 156, 158, 159.

DMS. Lot No. 31015 BREL Derby 1986–1987. –/62 1W (s –/48 1W) 24.2 t.
MS. Lot No. BREL Derby 31037 1987. –/73 (s –/58) 22.6 t.
DMSL. Lot No. BREL Derby 31016 1986–1987. –/60 1T (s –/45 1T) 25.0 t.

s – Refurbished Arriva Trains Northern units. Fitted with 2+2 high back Richmond seating.

Note: The centre cars of the 3-car units are owned by West Yorkshire PTE, although managed by Porterbrook Leasing Company.

144 001	s	**YP**	P	*AN*	NL	55801	55824
144 002	s	**YP**	P	*AN*	NL	55802	55825
144 003	s	**YP**	P	*AN*	NL	55803	55826
144 004	s	**YP**	P	*AN*	NL	55804	55827
144 005	s	**YP**	P	*AN*	NL	55805	55828
144 006	s	**YP**	P	*AN*	NL	55806	55829
144 007	s	**YP**	P	*AN*	NL	55807	55830
144 008	s	**YP**	P	*AN*	NL	55808	55831
144 009	s	**YP**	P	*AN*	NL	55809	55832
144 010	s	**YP**	P	*AN*	NL	55810	55833
144 011	s	**YP**	P	*AN*	NL	55811	55834
144 012	s	**YP**	P	*AN*	NL	55812	55835
144 013	s	**YP**	P	*AN*	NL	55813	55836
144 014	s	**YP**	P	*AN*	NL	55814	55850	55837
144 015	s	**YP**	P	*AN*	NL	55815	55851	55838
144 016		**WY**	P	*AN*	NL	55816	55852	55839
144 017		**WY**	P	*AN*	NL	55817	55853	55840
144 018		**WY**	P	*AN*	NL	55818	55854	55841
144 019		**WY**	P	*AN*	NL	55819	55855	55842
144 020		**WY**	P	*AN*	NL	55820	55856	55843
144 021		**WY**	P	*AN*	NL	55821	55857	55844
144 022	s	**YP**	P	*AN*	NL	55822	55858	55845
144 023	s	**YP**	P	*AN*	NL	55823	55859	55846

Name (carried on DMSL):

144 001 THE PENISTONE LINE PARTNERSHIP

CLASS 150/0   SPRINTER   BREL YORK

DMSL–MS–DMS. Prototype Sprinter.

Construction: Steel.
Engines: One Cummins NT-855-R4 of 213 kW (285 h.p.) at 2100 r.p.m.
Bogies: BX8P (powered), BX8T (non-powered).
Couplers: BSI at outer end of driving vehicles, bar non-driving ends.
Seating Layout: 3+2 (mainly unidirectional).
Dimensions: 20.06/20.18 x 2.82 m.
Gangways: Within unit only.   **Wheel Arrangement:** 2-B – 2-B – B-2.
Doors: Single-leaf sliding.   **Maximum Speed:** 75 m.p.h.
Multiple Working: Within class and with Classes 142, 143, 144, 153, 155, 156, 158, 159, 170.

DMSL. Lot No. 30984 1984. –/72 1T. 35.8 t.
MS. Lot No. 30986 1984. –/92. 34.4 t.
DMSL. Lot No. 30985 1984. –/76. 35.6 t.

150 001	r	**CO**	A	*CT*	TS	55200	55400	55300
150 002	r	**CO**	A	*CT*	TS	55201	55401	55301

CLASS 150/1   SPRINTER   BREL YORK

DMSL–DMS or DMSL–DMSL–DMS or DMSL–DMS–DMS.

Construction: Steel.
Engines: One Cummins NT855R5 of 213 kW (285 h.p.) at 2100 r.p.m.
Bogies: BP38 (powered), BT38 (non-powered).
Couplers: BSI.
Seating Layout: 3+2 facing as built but 150 010–150 132 were reseated with mainly unidirectional seating.
Dimensions: 19.74 x 2.82 m.
Gangways: Within unit only.   **Wheel Arrangement:** 2-B (– 2-B) – B-2.
Doors: Single-leaf sliding.   **Maximum Speed:** 75 m.p.h.
Multiple Working: Within class and with Classes 142, 143, 144, 153, 155, 156, 158, 159, 170.

DMSL. Lot No. 31011 1985–1986. –/72 1T (s –/59 1TD, t –/71 1W 1T, u –/71 1T). 36.5 t.
DMS. Lot No. 31012 1985–1986. –/76 (s –/65, u –/70). 38.45 t.

Non-standard livery: 150 134 is in plain dark blue.

Notes: The centre cars of the 3-car units are Class 150/2 vehicles. For details see Class 150/2.
Units in **NW** livery have been refurbished with new Chapman seating.

150 003	ru	**CO**	A	*CT*	TS	52103	57210	57103
150 005	ru	**CO**	A	*CT*	TS	52105	52210	57105
150 010	ru	**CO**	A	*CT*	TS	52110	57226	57110
150 011	ru	**CO**	A	*CT*	TS	52111	52204	57111
150 012	ru	**CO**	A	*CT*	TS	52112	57206	57112

▲ BR Green-liveried 101 685 arrives at Manchester Piccadilly with the 11.50 from Marple on 17/12/02. **Tony Miles**

▼ Chiltern Railways uses a refurbished Class 121 "Bubble car" on certain Princes Risborough–Aylesbury services. On 16/09/03 121 020 arrives at Princes Risborough with the 08.09 from Aylesbury. **Kim Fullbrook**

▲ Ex-works in new Merseytravel livery 142 052 leaves Sheffield with the 19.14 local service to Manchester Piccadilly on 14/07/02.   **Robert Pritchard**

▼ Valley Lines-liveried 143 601 passes Coedkernew, with the 12.35 Newport–Cardiff on 30/08/03.   **Paul Robertson**

▲ New West Yorkshire PTE-liveried 144 010 passes Normanton with a Sheffield–Leeds service on 11/11/02. **Simon Wright**

▼ Silverlink-liveried 150 130 arrives at Clapham Junction on 17/09/02 with a shuttle from Kensington Olympia, instead of the more usual Class 313. **Alex Dasi-Sutton**

Carrying one of the several Wessex Trains promotional liveries 150 266 nears Bathampton on 18/04/03 with the 14.57 Weymouth–Bristol. **John Chalcraft**

▲ Heart of Wales orange-liveried 153 321 is seen with 158 836 on the 06.30 Milford Haven–Liverpool on 30/08/03, near Abergavenny. **Paul Robertson**

▼ All Class 155s still retain the old West Yorkshire PTE livery. On 19/07/03 155 346 is seen at Knottingley after arrival with the 12.51 from Wakefield Westgate.
Robert Pritchard

ScotRail-liveried 156 456 passes Gilsland, the highest point on the Newcastle–Carlisle line, with the 12.36 Newcastle–Stranraer on 11/05/02. These services are manned by Arriva crews between Newcastle and Carlisle. **Dave McAlone**

▲ New First Group-liveried 156 420 leaves Warrington Bank Quay with a Liverpool service on 18/07/03. **Doug Birmingham**

▼ Arriva Trans-Pennine-liveried 158 781 passes the industrial surroundings of Melton Ross with the 12.32 Cleethorpes–Manchester Airport on 23/04/03.
Paul Robertson

▲ Central Trains reformed several of its Class 158 fleet into 3-car units again in 2003. On 13/07/03 158 954 is seen at Castle Bromwich Junction with a Nottingham–Cardiff service. **Gavin Morrison**

▼ South West Trains-liveried 159 022 and 159 014 pass new Malden on 12/04/03 with the 06.46 Honiton–Waterloo. **Alex Dasi-Sutton**

150 013	ru	CO	A	CT	TS	52113	52226	57113
150 014	ru	CO	A	CT	TS	52114	57204	57114
150 015	ru	CO	A	CT	TS	52115	52206	57115
150 016	ru	CO	A	CT	TS	52116	57212	57116
150 017	ru	CO	A	CT	TS	52117	57209	57117
150 018	ru	CO	A	CT	TS	52118	52220	57118
150 019	ru	CO	A	CT	TS	52119	57220	57119
150 101	ru	CO	A	CT	TS	52101	57101	
150 102	ru	CO	A	CT	TS	52102	57102	
150 104	ru	CO	A	CT	TS	52104	57104	
150 106	r	CO	A	CT	TS	52106	57106	
150 107	r	CO	A	CT	TS	52107	57107	
150 108	ru	CO	A	CT	TS	52108	57108	
150 109	ru	CO	A	CT	TS	52109	57109	
150 120	t	SL	A	SL	BY	52120	57120	
150 121	ru	CO	A	CT	TS	52121	57121	
150 122	ru	CO	A	CT	TS	52122	57122	
150 123	t	SL	A	SL	BY	52123	57123	
150 124	ru	CO	A	CT	TS	52124	57124	
150 125	ru	CO	A	CT	TS	52125	57125	
150 126	ru	CO	A	CT	TS	52126	57126	
150 127	t	SL	A	SL	BY	52127	57127	Bletchley TMD
150 128	t	SL	A	SL	BY	52128	57128	Community Forest
150 129	t	SL	A	SL	BY	52129	57129	MARSTON VALE
150 130	t	SL	A	SL	BY	52130	57130	Bedford–Bletchley 150
150 131	t	SL	A	SL	BY	52131	57131	LESLIE CRABBE
150 132	r	CO	A	CT	TS	52132	57132	
150 133	s	NW	A	NW	NH	52133	57133	
150 134	s	O	A	NW	NH	52134	57134	
150 135	s	NW	A	NW	NH	52135	57135	
150 136	s	NW	A	NW	NH	52136	57136	
150 137	s	NW	A	NW	NH	52137	57137	
150 138	s	NW	A	NW	NH	52138	57138	
150 139	s	NW	A	NW	NH	52139	57139	
150 140	s	NW	A	NW	NH	52140	57140	
150 141	s	NW	A	NW	NH	52141	57141	
150 142	s	NW	A	NW	NH	52142	57142	
150 143	s	NW	A	NW	NH	52143	57143	
150 144	s	NW	A	NW	NH	52144	57144	
150 145	s	NW	A	NW	NH	52145	57145	
150 146	s	NW	A	NW	NH	52146	57146	
150 147	s	NW	A	NW	NH	52147	57147	
150 148	s	NW	A	NW	NH	52148	57148	
150 149	s	NW	A	NW	NH	52149	57149	
150 150	s	NW	A	NW	NH	52150	57150	

CLASS 150/2   SPRINTER   BREL YORK

DMSL–DMS.

Construction: Steel.
Engines: One Cummins NT855R5 of 213 kW (285 h.p.) at 2100 r.p.m.
Bogies: BP38 (powered), BT38 (non-powered).
Couplers: BSI.
Seating Layout: 3+2 mainly unidirectional seating.
Dimensions: 19.74 x 2.82 m.
Gangways: Throughout.   **Wheel Arrangement:** 2-B – B-2.
Doors: Single-leaf sliding.   **Maximum Speed:** 75 m.p.h.
Multiple Working: Within class and with Classes 142, 143, 144, 153, 155, 156, 158, 159, 170.

DMSL. Lot No. 31017 1986–1987. –/73 1T (s –/62 1TD, v –/60 1T, w –/66 1T). 35.8 t.
DMS. Lot No. 31018 1986–1987. –/76 (* –/68, s –/70, v –/56, w –/73). 34.9 t.

Units in **NW** livery have been refurbished with new Chapman seating.
v Refurbished Wales & Borders units with 2+2 individual Chapman seating.
w Refurbished Wessex Trains units with 2+2 individual Chapman seating.

150 201	s	**NW**	A	*NW*	NH	52201	57201	
150 202		**CO**	A	*CT*	TS	52202	57202	
150 203	s	**NW**	A	*NW*	NH	52203	57203	
150 205	s	**NW**	A	*NW*	NH	52205	57205	
150 207	s	**NW**	A	*NW*	NH	52207	57207	
150 208		**SR**	P	*SR*	HA	52208	57208	
150 211	s	**NW**	A	*NW*	NH	52211	57211	
150 213	r*	**AR**	P	*AR*	NC	52213	57213	LORD NELSON
150 214		**CO**	A	*CT*	TS	52214	57214	
150 215	s	**NW**	A	*NW*	NH	52215	57215	
150 216		**CO**	A	*CT*	TS	52216	57216	
150 217	r*	**PS**	P	*AR*	NC	52217	57217	OLIVER CROMWELL
150 218	s	**NW**	A	*NW*	NH	52218	57218	
150 219	rw	**WZ**	P	*WX*	CF	52219	57219	
150 221	rw	**WZ**	P	*WX*	CF	52221	57221	
150 222	s	**NW**	A	*NW*	NH	52222	57222	
150 223	s	**NW**	A	*NW*	NH	52223	57223	
150 224	s	**NW**	A	*NW*	NH	52224	57224	
150 225	s	**NW**	A	*NW*	NH	52225	57225	
150 227	r*	**AR**	P	*AR*	NC	52227	57227	SIR ALF RAMSEY
150 228	tu	**RR**	P	*AN*	NL	52228	57228	
150 229	r*	**AR**	P	*AR*	NC	52229	57229	GEORGE BORROW
150 230	rw	**WZ**	P	*WX*	CF	52230	57230	The Tamar Kingfisher
150 231	r*	**PS**	P	*AR*	NC	52231	57231	KING EDMUND
150 232	rw	**WZ**	P	*WX*	CF	52232	57232	The Coastal Connection
150 233	rw	**WZ**	P	*WX*	CF	52233	57233	The Lady Margaret of Looe Valley
150 234	rw	**WZ**	P	*WX*	CF	52234	57234	The National Trust
150 235	r*	**AR**	P	*AR*	NC	52235	57235	CARDINAL WOLSEY

150 236	rw	**WZ**	P	*WX*	CF	52236	57236	
150 237	r*	**AR**	P	*AR*	NC	52237	57237	HEREWARD THE WAKE
150 238	rw	**WZ**	P	*WX*	CF	52238	57238	Exeter Explorer
150 239	rw	**WZ**	P	*WX*	CF	52239	57239	
150 240	rw	**WZ**	P	*WX*	CF	52240	57240	
150 241	rw	**WZ**	P	*WX*	CF	52241	57241	The Tarka Belle
150 242	rw	**WZ**	P	*WX*	CF	52242	57242	
150 243	rw	**WZ**	P	*WX*	CF	52243	57243	
150 244	rw	**WZ**	P	*WX*	CF	52244	57244	The West Cornwall Experience
150 245	r	**AR**	P	*AR*	NC	52245	57245	
150 246	rw	**WZ**	P	*WX*	CF	52246	57246	
150 247	rw	**WZ**	P	*WX*	CF	52247	57247	
150 248	rw	**WZ**	P	*WX*	CF	52248	57248	The Great Gardens of Cornwall
150 249	rw	**WZ**	P	*WX*	CF	52249	57249	
150 250		**SR**	P	*SR*	HA	52250	57250	
150 251	rw	**WZ**	P	*WX*	CF	52251	57251	
150 252		**SR**	P	*SR*	HA	52252	57252	
150 253	rw	**WZ**	P	*WX*	CF	52253	57253	The Exmouth Avocet
150 254	rw	**WZ**	P	*WX*	CF	52254	57254	
150 255	r*	**AR**	P	*AR*	NC	52255	57255	HENRY BLOGG
150 256		**SR**	P	*SR*	HA	52256	57256	
150 257	r*	**AR**	P	*AR*	NC	52257	57257	QUEEN BOADICEA
150 258		**SR**	P	*SR*	HA	52258	57258	
150 259		**SR**	P	*SR*	HA	52259	57259	
150 260		**SR**	P	*SR*	HA	52260	57260	
150 261	rw	**WZ**	P	*WX*	CF	52261	57261	The Riviera Flyer
150 262		**SR**	P	*SR*	HA	52262	57262	
150 263	rw	**WZ**	P	*WX*	CF	52263	57263	The Castles of Cornwall
150 264		**SR**	P	*SR*	HA	52264	57264	
150 265	rw	**WZ**	P	*WX*	CF	52265	57265	The Falmouth Flyer
150 266	rw	**WZ**	P	*WX*	CF	52266	57266	The Whitley Wonder
150 267	rv	**VW**	P	*WB*	CF	52267	57267	
150 268		**RR**	P	*AN*	NL	52268	57268	
150 269		**RR**	P	*AN*	NL	52269	57269	
150 270		**RR**	P	*AN*	NL	52270	57270	
150 271		**RR**	P	*AN*	NL	52271	57271	
150 272		**RR**	P	*AN*	NL	52272	57272	
150 273		**RR**	P	*AN*	NL	52273	57273	
150 274		**RR**	P	*AN*	NL	52274	57274	
150 275		**RR**	P	*AN*	NL	52275	57275	
150 276		**RR**	P	*AN*	NL	52276	57276	
150 277		**RR**	P	*AN*	NL	52277	57277	
150 278	rv	**VW**	P	*WB*	CF	52278	57278	
150 279	v	**VW**	P	*WB*	CF	52279	57279	
150 280	v	**VW**	P	*WB*	CF	52280	57280	University of Glamorgan/ Prifysgol Morgannwg
150 281	v	**VW**	P	*WB*	CF	52281	57281	
150 282	v	**VW**	P	*WB*	CF	52282	57282	

150 283	**SR**	P	*SR*	HA	52283	57283
150 284	**SR**	P	*SR*	HA	52284	57284
150 285	**SR**	P	*SR*	HA	52285	57285

CLASS 153 SUPER SPRINTER LEYLAND BUS

DMSL. Converted by Hunslet-Barclay, Kilmarnock from Class 155 2-car units.

Construction: Steel. Built from Leyland National bus parts on bogied underframes.
Engine: One Cummins NT855R5 of 213 kW (285 h.p.) at 2100 r.p.m.
Bogies: One P3-10 (powered) and one BT38 (non-powered).
Couplers: BSI.
Seating Layout: 2+2 facing/unidirectional.
Dimensions: 23.21 x 2.70 m.
Gangways: Throughout.   **Wheel Arrangement:** 2-B.
Doors: Single-leaf sliding plug.   **Maximum Speed:** 75 m.p.h.
Multiple Working: Within class and with Classes 142, 143, 144, 150, 155, 156, 158, 159, 170.

52301–52335. DMSL. Lot No. 31026 1987–1988. Converted under Lot No.31115 1991–2. –/75 1T 1W (* –/69 1T 1W). 41.2 t.
57301–57335. DMSL. Lot No. 31027 1987–1988. Converted under Lot No.31115 1991–2. –/75 1T (* –/69 1T). 41.2 t.

Advertising Livery: 153 314 Norfolk and Norwich Festival (Black and orange).

Notes: Cars numbered in the 573xx series were renumbered by adding 50 to their original number so that the last two digits correspond with the set number. Central Trains and First North Western units have been fitted with new Chapman seating.
Arriva Trains Northern units have been fitted with new Richmond seating.
Wales & Borders/Wessex Trains units have been reseated with seats removed from that company's Class 158 units.
Anglia Railways units have Chapman seating and a bicycle rack.

153 301		**AV**	A	*AN*	NL	52301	
153 302	r	**DC**	A	*WX*	CF	52302	
153 303	r	**HW**	A	*WB*	CF	52303	
153 304		**AV**	A	*AN*	NL	52304	
153 305	r	**WX**	A	*WX*	CF	52305	
153 306	r*	**PS**	P	*AR*	NC	52306	EDITH CAVELL
153 307	r	**AV**	A	*AN*	NL	52307	
153 308	r	**DC**	A	*WX*	CF	52308	
153 309	r*	**PS**	P	*AR*	NC	52309	GERARD FIENNES
153 310		**NW**	P	*WB*	CF	52310	
153 311	r*	**PS**	P	*AR*	NC	52311	JOHN CONSTABLE
153 312	r	**HW**	A	*WB*	CF	52312	
153 313		**NW**	P	*WB*	CF	52313	
153 314	r*	**AL**	P	*AR*	NC	52314	DELIA SMITH
153 315		**AV**	A	*AN*	NL	52315	
153 316		**NW**	P	*NW*	NH	52316	
153 317		**AV**	A	*AN*	NL	52317	

153 318	r	**WX**	A	*WX*	CF	52318
153 319		**AV**	A	*AN*	NL	52319
153 320	r	**HW**	P	*WB*	CF	52320
153 321	r	**HW**	P	*WB*	CF	52321
153 322	r*	**AR**	P	*AR*	NC	52322
153 323	r	**HW**	P	*WB*	CF	52323
153 324		**NW**	P	*NW*	NH	52324
153 325	r	**RR**	P	*CT*	TS	52325
153 326	r*	**PS**	P	*AR*	NC	52326
153 327	r	**HW**	A	*WB*	CF	52327
153 328		**AV**	A	*AN*	NL	52328
153 329	r	**RR**	P	*WX*	CF	52329
153 330		**NW**	P	*NW*	NH	52330
153 331		**AV**	A	*AN*	NL	52331
153 332		**NW**	P	*NW*	NH	52332
153 333	r	**RR**	P	*CT*	TS	52333
153 334	r	**RR**	P	*CT*	TS	52334
153 335	r*	**AR**	P	*AR*	NC	52335
153 351		**AV**	A	*AN*	NL	57351
153 352		**AV**	A	*AN*	NL	57352
153 353	r	**HW**	A	*WB*	CF	57353
153 354	r	**RR**	P	*CT*	TS	57354
153 355	r	**WX**	A	*WX*	CF	57355
153 356	r	**RR**	P	*CT*	TS	57356
153 357		**AV**	A	*AN*	NL	57357
153 358		**NW**	P	*NW*	NH	57358
153 359		**NW**	P	*NW*	NH	57359
153 360		**NW**	P	*NW*	NH	57360
153 361		**NW**	P	*WB*	CF	57361
153 362	r	**HW**	A	*WB*	CF	57362
153 363		**NW**	P	*NW*	NH	57363
153 364	r	**RR**	P	*CT*	TS	57364
153 365	r	**RR**	P	*CT*	TS	57365
153 366	r	**RR**	P	*CT*	TS	57366
153 367		**NW**	P	*WB*	CF	57367
153 368	r	**WX**	A	*WX*	CF	57368
153 369	r	**RR**	P	*WX*	CF	57369
153 370	r	**WX**	A	*WX*	CF	57370
153 371	r	**RR**	P	*CT*	TS	57371
153 372	r	**WX**	A	*WX*	CF	57372
153 373	r	**WX**	A	*WX*	CF	57373
153 374	r	**DC**	A	*WX*	CF	57374
153 375	r	**RR**	P	*CT*	TS	57375
153 376	r	**RR**	P	*CT*	TS	57376
153 377	r	**DC**	A	*WX*	CF	57377
153 378		**AV**	A	*AN*	NL	57378
153 379	r	**RR**	P	*CT*	TS	57379
153 380	r	**DC**	A	*WX*	CF	57380
153 381	r	**RR**	P	*CT*	TS	57381
153 382	r	**DC**	A	*WX*	CF	57382
153 383	r	**RR**	P	*CT*	TS	57383

BENJAMIN BRITTEN

TED ELLIS

MICHAEL PALIN

Dylan Thomas 1914–1953

153 384	r	**RR**	P	*CT*	TS	57384
153 385	r	**RR**	P	*CT*	TS	57385

CLASS 155 SUPER SPRINTER LEYLAND BUS

DMSL–DMS.

Construction: Steel. Built from Leyland National bus parts on bogied underframes.
Engines: One Cummins NT855R5 of 213 kW (285 h.p.) at 2100 r.p.m.
Bogies: One P3-10 (powered) and one BT38 (non-powered).
Couplers: BSI.
Seating Layout: 2+2 facing/unidirectional.
Dimensions: 23.21 x 2.70 m.
Gangways: Throughout.   **Wheel Arrangement:** 2-B – B-2.
Doors: Single-leaf sliding plug.   **Maximum Speed:** 75 m.p.h.
Multiple Working: Within class and with Classes 142, 143, 144, 150, 153, 156, 158, 159, 170.

DMSL. Lot No. 31057 1988. –/80 1TD 1W. 39.0 t.
DMS. Lot No. 31058 1988. –/80. 38.7 t.

Note: These units are owned by West Yorkshire PTE, although managed by Porterbrook Leasing Company.

155 341	**WY**	P	*AN*	NL	52341	57341
155 342	**WY**	P	*AN*	NL	52342	57342
155 343	**WY**	P	*AN*	NL	52343	57343
155 344	**WY**	P	*AN*	NL	52344	57344
155 345	**WY**	P	*AN*	NL	52345	57345
155 346	**WY**	P	*AN*	NL	52346	57346
155 347	**WY**	P	*AN*	NL	52347	57347

CLASS 156 SUPER SPRINTER METRO-CAMMELL

DMSL–DMS.

Construction: Steel.
Engines: One Cummins NT855R5 of 213 kW (285 h.p.) at 2100 r.p.m.
Bogies: One P3-10 (powered) and one BT38 (non-powered).
Couplers: BSI.
Seating Layout: 2+2 facing/unidirectional.
Dimensions: 23.03 x 2.73 m.
Gangways: Throughout.   **Wheel Arrangement:** 2-B – B-2.
Doors: Single-leaf sliding plug.   **Maximum Speed:** 75 m.p.h.
Multiple Working: Within class and with Classes 142, 143, 144, 150, 153, 155, 158, 159, 170.

DMSL. Lot No. 31028 1988–1989. –/74 (†* –/72, st –/70, u –/68) 1TD 1W. 36.1 t.
DMS. Lot No. 31029 1987–1989. –/76 (q –/78, † –/74, tu –/72) 35.5 t.

Notes: 156 500–156 514 are owned by Strathclyde PTE, although managed by Angel.
Central Trains and First North Western units have been fitted with new Chapman seating.
Arriva Trains Northern units have been fitted with new Richmond seating.

156 401	r*	**CT**	P	*CT*	TS	52401	57401
156 402	r*	**P**	P	*CT*	TS	52402	57402
156 403	r*	**RE**	P	*CT*	TS	52403	57403
156 404	r*	**RE**	P	*CT*	TS	52404	57404
156 405	r*	**RE**	P	*CT*	TS	52405	57405
156 406	r*	**RE**	P	*CT*	TS	52406	57406
156 407	r*	**CT**	P	*CT*	TS	52407	57407
156 408	r*	**RE**	P	*CT*	TS	52408	57408
156 409	r*	**RE**	P	*CT*	TS	52409	57409
156 410	r*	**CT**	P	*CT*	TS	52410	57410
156 411	r*	**RE**	P	*CT*	TS	52411	57411
156 412	r*	**RE**	P	*CT*	TS	52412	57412
156 413	r*	**RE**	P	*CT*	TS	52413	57413
156 414	r*	**RE**	P	*CT*	TS	52414	57414
156 415	r*	**RE**	P	*CT*	TS	52415	57415
156 416	r*	**RE**	P	*CT*	TS	52416	57416
156 417	r*	**RE**	P	*CT*	TS	52417	57417
156 418	r*	**RE**	P	*CT*	TS	52418	57418
156 419	r*	**RE**	P	*CT*	TS	52419	57419
156 420	s	**FS**	P	*NW*	NH	52420	57420	LA' AL RATTY Ravenglass & Eskdale Railway
156 421	s	**RN**	P	*NW*	NH	52421	57421
156 422	r*	**RE**	P	*CT*	TS	52422	57422
156 423	s	**FS**	P	*NW*	NH	52423	57423
156 424	s	**RN**	P	*NW*	NH	52424	57424
156 425	s	**RN**	P	*NW*	NH	52425	57425
156 426	s	**RN**	P	*NW*	NH	52426	57426
156 427	s	**FS**	P	*NW*	NH	52427	57427
156 428	s	**RN**	P	*NW*	NH	52428	57428
156 429	s	**RN**	P	*NW*	NH	52429	57429
156 430	t	**SC**	A	*SR*	CK	52430	57430
156 431	t	**SC**	A	*SR*	CK	52431	57431
156 432	t	**SC**	A	*SR*	CK	52432	57432
156 433	t	**SC**	A	*SR*	CK	52433	57433	The Kilmarnock Edition
156 434	t	**SC**	A	*SR*	CK	52434	57434
156 435	t	**SC**	A	*SR*	CK	52435	57435
156 436	†	**SC**	A	*SR*	CK	52436	57436
156 437	rt	**SC**	A	*SR*	CK	52437	57437
156 438	q	**NS**	A	*AN*	NL	52438	57438
156 439	rt	**SC**	A	*SR*	CK	52439	57439
156 440	s	**RN**	P	*NW*	NH	52440	57440
156 441	s	**RN**	P	*NW*	NH	52441	57441
156 442	rt	**SC**	A	*SR*	CK	52442	57442
156 443	q	**NS**	A	*AN*	HT	52443	57443
156 444	q	**NS**	A	*AN*	HT	52444	57444

156 445	u	**SC**	A	*SR*	CK	52445	57445
156 446	rt	**SR**	A	*SR*	CK	52446	57446
156 447	ru	**SR**	A	*SR*	CK	52447	57447
156 448	q	**NS**	A	*AN*	HT	52448	57448
156 449	ru	**SR**	A	*SR*	CK	52449	57449
156 450	t	**SR**	A	*SR*	CK	52450	57450
156 451	q	**NS**	A	*AN*	HT	52451	57451
156 452	s	**FS**	P	*NW*	NH	52452	57452
156 453	ru	**SR**	A	*SR*	CK	52453	57453
156 454	q	**NS**	A	*AN*	HT	52454	57454
156 455	s	**RN**	P	*NW*	NH	52455	57455
156 456	rt	**SR**	A	*SR*	CK	52456	57456
156 457	rt	**SR**	A	*SR*	CK	52457	57457
156 458	rt	**SR**	A	*SR*	CK	52458	57458
156 459	s	**RN**	P	*NW*	NH	52459	57459
156 460	s	**RN**	P	*NW*	NH	52460	57460
156 461	s	**RN**	P	*NW*	NH	52461	57461
156 462	r	**SR**	A	*SR*	CK	52462	57462
156 463	q	**NS**	A	*AN*	HT	52463	57463
156 464	s	**RN**	P	*NW*	NH	52464	57464
156 465	u	**SR**	A	*SR*	CK	52465	57465
156 466	s	**RN**	P	*NW*	NH	52466	57466
156 467	r	**SR**	A	*SR*	CK	52467	57467
156 468	q	**NS**	A	*AN*	NL	52468	57468
156 469	q	**NS**	A	*AN*	HT	52469	57469
156 470	q	**NS**	A	*AN*	NL	52470	57470
156 471	q	**NS**	A	*AN*	NL	52471	57471
156 472	q	**NS**	A	*AN*	NL	52472	57472
156 473	q	**NS**	A	*AN*	NL	52473	57473
156 474	rt	**SR**	A	*SR*	CK	52474	57474
156 475	q	**NS**	A	*AN*	NL	52475	57475
156 476	rt	**SR**	A	*SR*	CK	52476	57476
156 477	rt	**SR**	A	*SR*	CK	52477	57477
156 478	t	**SR**	A	*SR*	CK	52478	57478
156 479	q	**NS**	A	*AN*	NL	52479	57479
156 480	q	**NS**	A	*AN*	NL	52480	57480
156 481	q	**NS**	A	*AN*	NL	52481	57481
156 482	q	**NS**	A	*AN*	NL	52482	57482
156 483	q	**NS**	A	*AN*	NL	52483	57483
156 484	q	**NS**	A	*AN*	NL	52484	57484
156 485	ru	**SR**	A	*SR*	CK	52485	57485
156 486	q	**NS**	A	*AN*	NL	52486	57486
156 487	q	**NS**	A	*AN*	NL	52487	57487
156 488	q	**NS**	A	*AN*	NL	52488	57488
156 489	q	**NS**	A	*AN*	NL	52489	57489
156 490	q	**NS**	A	*AN*	NL	52490	57490
156 491	q	**NS**	A	*AN*	NL	52491	57491
156 492	rt	**SR**	A	*SR*	CK	52492	57492
156 493	rt	**SR**	A	*SR*	CK	52493	57493
156 494	§	**SC**	A	*SR*	CK	52494	57494
156 495	ru	**SC**	A	*SR*	CK	52495	57495

156 496	ru	**SR**	A	*SR*	CK	52496	57496
156 497	q	**NS**	A	*AN*	NL	52497	57497
156 498	q	**NS**	A	*AN*	NL	52498	57498
156 499	rt	**SR**	A	*SR*	CK	52499	57499
156 500	u	**SC**	A	*SR*	CK	52500	57500
156 501		**SC**	A	*SR*	CK	52501	57501
156 502		**SC**	A	*SR*	CK	52502	57502
156 503		**SC**	A	*SR*	CK	52503	57503
156 504		**SC**	A	*SR*	CK	52504	57504
156 505		**SC**	A	*SR*	CK	52505	57505
156 506		**SC**	A	*SR*	CK	52506	57506
156 507		**SC**	A	*SR*	CK	52507	57507
156 508		**SC**	A	*SR*	CK	52508	57508
156 509		**SC**	A	*SR*	CK	52509	57509
156 510		**SC**	A	*SR*	CK	52510	57510
156 511		**SC**	A	*SR*	CK	52511	57511
156 512		**SC**	A	*SR*	CK	52512	57512
156 513		**SC**	A	*SR*	CK	52513	57513
156 514		**SC**	A	*SR*	CK	52514	57514

CLASS 158/0   BREL

DMSL(B)–DMSL(A) or DMCL–DMSL or DMCL–MSL–DMSL.

Construction: Welded aluminium.
Engines: 158 701–158 814: One Cummins NTA855R of 260 kW (350 h.p.) at 1900 r.p.m.
158 863–158 872: One Cummins NTA855R of 300 kW (400 h.p.) at 2100 r.p.m.
158 815–158 862: One Perkins 2006-TWH of 260 kW (350 h.p.) at 1900 r.p.m.
Bogies: One BREL P4 (powered) and one BREL T4 (non-powered) per car.
Couplers: BSI.
Seating Layout: 2+2 facing/unidirectional in all standard and first class unless stated. 2+1 facing/unidirectional in 158 747–158 751 first class (declassified in Wessex Trains units).
Dimensions: 22.57 x 2.70 m.
Gangways: Throughout.   **Wheel Arrangement:** 2-B – B-2.
Doors: Twin-leaf swing plug.   **Maximum Speed:** 90 m.p.h.
Multiple Working: Within class and with Classes 142, 143, 144, 150, 153, 155, 156, 159, 170.

DMSL(B). Lot No. 31051 BREL Derby 1989–1992. –/68 1TD 1W. († –/66 1TD 1W, t –/64 1TD 1W). Public telephone and trolley space. 38.5 t.
MSL. Lot No. 31050 BREL Derby 1991. 37.1 t. –/70 2T. 37.1 t.
DMSL(A). Lot No. 31052 BREL Derby 1989–1992. –/70 1T († –/68 1T, t –/66 1T). 37.8 t.

The above details refer to the "as built" condition. The following DMSL(B) have now been converted to DMCL as follows:

52701–52744 (ScotRail/Arriva Trains Northern). Dia. DP318. 15/51 1TD 1W (* 15/53 1TD 1W).

52747–52751. (Arriva Trains Northern/Wessex Trains). Dia. DP323. 9/51 1TD 1W.
52760–52779/52781. (Arriva Trains Northern 2-car Units). Dia. DP331. 16/48 1TD 1W.
52798–52814 (Arriva Trains Northern 3-car Units). Dia. DP332. 32/32 1TD 1W.

Notes:
s – Arriva Trains Northern (Trans–Pennine) and Central Trains units have been refurbished with new shape seat cushions.
Arriva Trans–Pennine units also fitted with table lamps in first class.
t – Wales & Borders "Cambrian Line" units with some seats removed for additional luggage space. Central Trains style seats (code s) retained.
† – Wessex Trains and Wales & Borders units fitted with new Chapman seating.

All ScotRail 158s are "fitted" for RETB. When a unit arrives at Inverness the cab display unit is clipped on and plugged in.

Advertising Livery: 158 842 – Western Daily Mail (Silver, white and red with various images).

158 701	*	**SR**	P	*SR*	IS	52701	57701
158 702	*	**SR**	P	*SR*	IS	52702	57702	BBC Scotland – 75 Years
158 703	*	**SR**	P	*SR*	IS	52703	57703
158 704	*	**SR**	P	*SR*	IS	52704	57704
158 705	*	**SR**	P	*SR*	IS	52705	57705
158 706	*	**SR**	P	*SR*	IS	52706	57706
158 707	*	**SR**	P	*SR*	IS	52707	57707	Far North Line 125th ANNIVERSARY
158 708	*	**SR**	P	*SR*	IS	52708	57708
158 709	*	**SR**	P	*SR*	IS	52709	57709
158 710	*	**SR**	P	*SR*	IS	52710	57710
158 711	*	**SR**	P	*SR*	IS	52711	57711
158 712	*	**SR**	P	*SR*	IS	52712	57712
158 713	*	**SR**	P	*SR*	IS	52713	57713
158 714	*	**SR**	P	*SR*	IS	52714	57714
158 715	*	**SR**	P	*SR*	IS	52715	57715	Haymarket
158 716	*	**SR**	P	*SR*	IS	52716	57716
158 717	*	**SR**	P	*SR*	IS	52717	57717
158 718	*	**SR**	P	*SR*	IS	52718	57718
158 719	*	**SR**	P	*SR*	IS	52719	57719
158 720	*	**SR**	P	*SR*	IS	52720	57720
158 721	*	**SR**	P	*SR*	HA	52721	57721
158 722	*	**SR**	P	*SR*	HA	52722	57722
158 723	*	**SR**	P	*SR*	HA	52723	57723
158 724	*	**SR**	P	*SR*	HA	52724	57724
158 725	*	**SR**	P	*SR*	HA	52725	57725
158 726	*	**SR**	P	*SR*	HA	52726	57726
158 727	*	**SR**	P	*SR*	HA	52727	57727
158 728	*	**SR**	P	*SR*	HA	52728	57728
158 729	*	**SR**	P	*SR*	HA	52729	57729
158 730	*	**SR**	P	*SR*	HA	52730	57730
158 731	*	**SR**	P	*SR*	HA	52731	57731

158 732	*	**SR**	P	*SR*	HA	52732	57732
158 733	*	**SR**	P	*SR*	HA	52733	57733
158 734	*	**SR**	P	*SR*	HA	52734	57734
158 735	*	**SR**	P	*SR*	HA	52735	57735
158 736	*	**SR**	P	*SR*	HA	52736	57736
158 737		**TX**	P	*AN*	NL	52737	57737
158 738	*	**SR**	P	*SR*	HA	52738	57738
158 739	*	**SR**	P	*SR*	HA	52739	57739
158 740	*	**SR**	P	*SR*	HA	52740	57740
158 741	*	**SR**	P	*SR*	HA	52741	57741
158 742		**TX**	P	*AN*	NL	52742	57742
158 743		**TX**	P	*AN*	NL	52743	57743
158 744		**TX**	P	*AN*	NL	52744	57744
158 745	†	**WT**	P	*WX*	CF	52745	57745
158 746	†	**WT**	P	*WX*	CF	52746	57746	Spirit of the South West
158 747		**RE**	P	*WX*	CF	52747	57747
158 748		**RE**	P	*WX*	CF	52748	57748
158 749		**RE**	P	*WX*	CF	52749	57749
158 750		**RE**	P	*AN*	NL	52750	57750
158 751		**RE**	P	*WX*	CF	52751	57751
158 752		**NW**	P	*NW*	NH	52752	57752
158 753		**NW**	P	*NW*	NH	52753	57753
158 754		**NW**	P	*NW*	NH	52754	57754
158 755		**NW**	P	*NW*	NH	52755	57755
158 756		**NW**	P	*NW*	NH	52756	57756
158 757		**NW**	P	*NW*	NH	52757	57757
158 758		**NW**	P	*NW*	NH	52758	57758
158 759		**NW**	P	*NW*	NH	52759	57759
158 760	s	**TX**	P	*AN*	NL	52760	57760
158 761	s	**TX**	P	*AN*	NL	52761	57761
158 762	s	**TX**	P	*AN*	NL	52762	57762
158 763	s	**TX**	P	*AN*	NL	52763	57763
158 764	s	**TX**	P	*AN*	NL	52764	57764
158 765	s	**TX**	P	*AN*	NL	52765	57765
158 766	s	**TX**	P	*AN*	NL	52766	57766
158 767	s	**TX**	P	*AN*	NL	52767	57767
158 768	s	**TX**	P	*AN*	NL	52768	57768
158 769	s	**TX**	P	*AN*	NL	52769	57769
158 770	s	**TX**	P	*AN*	NL	52770	57770
158 771	s	**TX**	P	*AN*	HT	52771	57771
158 772	s	**TX**	P	*AN*	NL	52772	57772
158 773	s	**TX**	P	*AN*	NL	52773	57773
158 774	s	**TX**	P	*AN*	NL	52774	57774
158 775	s	**TX**	P	*AN*	HT	52775	57775
158 776	s	**TX**	P	*AN*	HT	52776	57776
158 777	s	**TX**	P	*AN*	HT	52777	57777
158 778	s	**TX**	P	*AN*	HT	52778	57778
158 779	s	**TX**	P	*AN*	HT	52779	57779
158 781	s	**TX**	P	*AN*	HT	52781	57781
158 782	s	**CT**	A	*CT*	TS	52782	57782
158 783	s	**CT**	A	*CT*	TS	52783	57783

158 787	s	**CT**	A	*CT*	TS	52787	57787	
158 788	s	**CT**	A	*CT*	TS	52788	57788	
158 791	s	**CT**	A	*CT*	TS	52791	57791	
158 798	s	**TX**	P	*AN*	HT	52798	58715	57798
158 799	s	**TX**	P	*AN*	HT	52799	58716	57799
158 800	s	**TX**	P	*AN*	HT	52800	58717	57800
158 801	s	**TX**	P	*AN*	HT	52801	58701	57801
158 802	s	**TX**	P	*AN*	HT	52802	58702	57802
158 803	s	**TX**	P	*AN*	HT	52803	58703	57803
158 804	s	**TX**	P	*AN*	HT	52804	58704	57804
158 805	s	**TX**	P	*AN*	HT	52805	58705	57805
158 806	s	**TX**	P	*AN*	HT	52806	58706	57806
158 807	s	**TX**	P	*AN*	HT	52807	58707	57807
158 808	s	**TX**	P	*AN*	HT	52808	58708	57808
158 809	s	**TX**	P	*AN*	HT	52809	58709	57809
158 810	s	**TX**	P	*AN*	HT	52810	58710	57810
158 811	s	**TX**	P	*AN*	HT	52811	58711	57811
158 812	s	**TX**	P	*AN*	HT	52812	58712	57812
158 813	s	**TX**	P	*AN*	HT	52813	58713	57813
158 814	s	**TX**	P	*AN*	HT	52814	58714	57814
158 815	†	**WT**	A	*WX*	CF	52815	57815	
158 816	†	**WT**	A	*WX*	CF	52816	57816	
158 817	†	**WB**	A	*WX*	CF	52817	57817	
158 818	†	**RE**	A	*WB*	CF	52818	57818	
158 819	†	**GP**	A	*WB*	CF	52819	57819	
158 820	†	**RE**	A	*WB*	CF	52820	57820	
158 821	†	**GP**	A	*WB*	CF	52821	57821	
158 822	†	**WB**	A	*WB*	CF	52822	57822	
158 823	†	**WB**	A	*WB*	CF	52823	57823	
158 824	†	**WB**	A	*WB*	CF	52824	57824	
158 825	†	**GP**	A	*WB*	CF	52825	57825	
158 826	†	**RE**	A	*WB*	CF	52826	57826	
158 827	†	**GP**	A	*WB*	CF	52827	57827	
158 828	†	**RE**	A	*WB*	CF	52828	57828	
158 829	†	**WB**	A	*WB*	CF	52829	57829	
158 830	†	**WB**	A	*WB*	CF	52830	57830	
158 831	†	**WB**	A	*WB*	CF	52831	57831	
158 832	†	**WB**	A	*WB*	CF	52832	57832	
158 833	†	**WB**	A	*WB*	CF	52833	57833	
158 834	†	**WB**	A	*WB*	CF	52834	57834	
158 835	†	**RE**	A	*WB*	CF	52835	57835	
158 836	†	**WB**	A	*WB*	CF	52836	57836	
158 837	†	**RE**	A	*WB*	CF	52837	57837	
158 838	†	**WB**	A	*WB*	CF	52838	57838	
158 839	†	**WB**	A	*WB*	CF	52839	57839	
158 840	†	**RE**	A	*WB*	CF	52840	57840	
158 841	†	**GP**	A	*WB*	CF	52841	57841	
158 842	†	**AL**	A	*WB*	CF	52842	57842	
158 843	†	**WB**	A	*WB*	CF	52843	57843	
158 844	rt	**CT**	A	*WB*	TS	52844	57844	
158 845	rt	**CT**	A	*WB*	TS	52845	57845	

158 846	rt	**CT**	A	*WB*	TS	52846	57846
158 847	rt	**CT**	A	*WB*	TS	52847	57847
158 848	rt	**CT**	A	*WB*	TS	52848	57848
158 849	rt	**CT**	A	*WB*	TS	52849	57849
158 850	rt	**CT**	A	*WB*	TS	52850	57850
158 851	rt	**CT**	A	*WB*	TS	52851	57851
158 852	rt	**CT**	A	*WB*	TS	52852	57852
158 853	rt	**CT**	A	*WB*	TS	52853	57853
158 854	rt	**CT**	A	*WB*	TS	52854	57854
158 855	s	**CT**	A	*WX*	CF	52855	57855
158 856	s	**CT**	A	*CT*	TS	52856	57856
158 857	s	**CT**	A	*CT*	TS	52857	57857
158 858	s	**CT**	A	*CT*	TS	52858	57858
158 859	s	**CT**	A	*CT*	TS	52859	57859
158 860	s	**CT**	A	*CT*	TS	52860	57860
158 861	s	**CT**	A	*CT*	TS	52861	57861
158 862	s	**CT**	A	*CT*	TS	52862	57862
158 863	†	**WT**	A	*WX*	CF	52863	57863
158 864	†	**WT**	A	*WX*	CF	52864	57864
158 865	†	**WT**	A	*WX*	CF	52865	57865
158 866	†	**WT**	A	*WX*	CF	52866	57866
158 867	†	**WT**	A	*WX*	CF	52867	57867
158 868	†	**WT**	A	*WX*	CF	52868	57868
158 869	†	**WT**	A	*WX*	CF	52869	57869
158 870	†	**WT**	A	*WX*	CF	52870	57870
158 871	†	**WT**	A	*WX*	CF	52871	57871
158 872	†	**WT**	A	*WX*	CF	52872	57872

CLASS 158/9   BREL

DMSL–DMS. Units leased by West Yorkshire PTE. Details as for Class 158/0 except for seating layout and toilets.

DMSL. Lot No. 31051 BREL Derby 1990–1992. –/70 1TD 1W. Public telephone and trolley space. 38.1 t.
DMS. Lot No. 31052 BREL Derby 1990–1992. –/72 and parcels area. 37.8 t.

Note: These units are leased by West Yorkshire PTE and are managed by Porterbrook Leasing Company.

158 901	**WY**	P	*AN*	NL	52901	57901
158 902	**YP**	P	*AN*	NL	52902	57902
158 903	**WY**	P	*AN*	NL	52903	57903
158 904	**WY**	P	*AN*	NL	52904	57904
158 905	**WY**	P	*AN*	NL	52905	57905
158 906	**WY**	P	*AN*	NL	52906	57906
158 907	**WY**	P	*AN*	NL	52907	57907
158 908	**WY**	P	*AN*	NL	52908	57908
158 909	**YN**	P	*AN*	NL	52909	57909
158 910	**YP**	P	*AN*	NL	52910	57910

CLASS 158/0   BREL

DMSL–DMSL–DMSL. 3-car units formed by Central Trains from former 2-car units. For details see above.

158 951	s	**CT**	A	*CT*	TS	57784	57780	52780
158 952	s	**CT**	A	*CT*	TS	52789	57785	52785
158 953	s	**CT**	A	*CT*	TS	52792	57790	52790
158 954	s	**CT**	A	*CT*	TS	52793	57786	52786
158 955	s	**CT**	A	*CT*	TS	57793	57794	52794
158 956	s	**CT**	A	*CT*	TS	52784	57795	52795
158 957	s	**CT**	A	*CT*	TS	57789	57796	52796
158 958	s	**CT**	A	*CT*	TS	57792	57797	52797

CLASS 159   BREL

DMCL–MSL–DMSL. Built as Class 158. Converted before entering passenger service to Class 159 by Rosyth Dockyard.

Construction: Welded aluminium.
Engines: One Cummins NTA855R of 300 kW (400 h.p.) at 2100 r.p.m.
Bogies: One BREL P4 (powered) and one BREL T4 (non-powered) per car.
Couplers: BSI.
Seating Layout: 1: 2+1 facing, 2: 2+2 facing/unidirectional.
Dimensions: 23.21 x 2.82 m.
Gangways: Throughout.   **Wheel Arrangement:** 2-B – B-2 – B-2.
Doors: Twin-leaf swing plug.   **Maximum Speed:** 90 m.p.h.
Multiple Working: Within class and with Classes 142, 143, 144, 150, 153, 155, 156, 158, 170.

DMCL. Lot No. 31051 BREL Derby 1992–1993. 24/28 1TD 1W. 38.5 t.
MSL. Lot No. 31050 BREL Derby 1992–1993. 38.0 t. –/72 1T and parcels area.
DMSL. Lot No. 31052 BREL Derby 1992–1993. –/72 1T and parcels area. 37.8 t.

159 001	**SW**	P	*SW*	SA	52873	58718	57873	CITY OF EXETER
159 002	**SW**	P	*SW*	SA	52874	58719	57874	CITY OF SALISBURY
159 003	**SW**	P	*SW*	SA	52875	58720	57875	TEMPLECOMBE
159 004	**SW**	P	*SW*	SA	52876	58721	57876	BASINGSTOKE AND DEANE
159 005	**SW**	P	*SW*	SA	52877	58722	57877	
159 006	**SW**	P	*SW*	SA	52878	58723	57878	
159 007	**SW**	P	*SW*	SA	52879	58724	57879	
159 008	**SW**	P	*SW*	SA	52880	58725	57880	
159 009	**SW**	P	*SW*	SA	52881	58726	57881	
159 010	**SW**	P	*SW*	SA	52882	58727	57882	
159 011	**SW**	P	*SW*	SA	52883	58728	57883	
159 012	**SW**	P	*SW*	SA	52884	58729	57884	
159 013	**SW**	P	*SW*	SA	52885	58730	57885	
159 014	**SW**	P	*SW*	SA	52886	58731	57886	
159 015	**SW**	P	*SW*	SA	52887	58732	57887	
159 016	**SW**	P	*SW*	SA	52888	58733	57888	

159 017	**SW** P *SW* SA	52889	58734	57889
159 018	**SW** P *SW* SA	52890	58735	57890
159 019	**SW** P *SW* SA	52891	58736	57891
159 020	**SW** P *SW* SA	52892	58737	57892
159 021	**SW** P *SW* SA	52893	58738	57893
159 022	**SW** P *SW* SA	52894	58739	57894

CLASS 165/0   NETWORK TURBO   BREL

DMCL–DMS (Thames Trains units) or DMSL–DMS and DMSL–MS–DMS (Chiltern units). Chiltern Railways units are being refurbished and fitted with air-conditioning.

Construction: Welded aluminium.
Engines: One Perkins 2006-TWH of 260 kW (350 h.p.) at 1900 r.p.m.
Bogies: BREL P3-17 (powered), BREL T3-17 (non-powered).
Couplers: BSI.
Seating Layout: 1: 2+2 facing (Thames Trains units only), 2: Thames Trains/Chiltern unrefurbished units: 3+2 facing/unidirectional. 2: Refurbished Chiltern units: 2+2 facing/unidirectional (DMSL and DMS) and 3+2 facing/unidirectional (MS).
Dimensions: 23.50 x 2.85 m.
Gangways: Within unit only.   **Wheel Arrangement:** 2-B (– B-2) – B-2.
Doors: Twin-leaf swing plug.   **Maximum Speed:** 75 m.p.h.
Multiple Working: Within class and with Classes 166 and 168.

58801–58805. DMCL (Thames Trains units). Lot No. 31087 BREL York 1990. 16/72 1T. 37.0 t.
58806–58812, 58814–58822 and 58873–58878. DMSL (Chiltern 2-car units – first class declassified). Lot No. 31087 BREL York 1990. 16/72 1T (* –/89 1T). 37.0 t.
58823–58833. DMSL (Chiltern 3-car units – first class declassified). Lot No. 31089 BREL York 1991–1992. 24/60 1T (* –/89 1T). 37.0 t.
58813. DMSL (Trial refurbished Chiltern vehicle). Lot No. 31087 BREL York 1990. –/82 1T. 37.0 t.
55404–55414. MS (Centre car of Chiltern 3-car units. Accommodation is unchanged by refurbishment). Lot No. 31090 BREL York 1991–1992. –/106. 37.0 t.
58834–58838. DMS (Thames Trains units). Lot No. 31088 BREL York 1991–1992. –/98. 37.0 t.
58839–58872. DMS (Chiltern units). Lot No. 31088 BREL York 1991–1992. –/98 (* –/94). 37.0 t.

Notes:

† Trial refurbished Chiltern Railways unit.
* Fully refurbished Chiltern Railways units.
165 006–165 039 are fitted with tripcocks for working over London Underground tracks between Harrow-on-the-Hill and Amersham.
Chiltern units had their first class seats declassified from 5 January 2003.

165 001		**NT**	A		RG	58801		58834
165 002		**NT**	A	*TT*	RG	58802		58835
165 003		**NT**	A	*TT*	RG	58803		58836
165 004		**NT**	A	*TT*	RG	58804		58837
165 005		**TT**	A	*TT*	RG	58805		58838
165 006		**NT**	A	*CR*	AL	58806		58839
165 007		**NT**	A	*CR*	AL	58807		58840
165 008		**NT**	A	*CR*	AL	58808		58841
165 009		**NT**	A	*CR*	AL	58809		58842
165 010		**NT**	A	*CR*	AL	58810		58843
165 011		**NT**	A	*CR*	AL	58811		58844
165 012		**NT**	A	*CR*	AL	58812		58845
165 013	†	**CR**	A	*CR*	AL	58813		58846
165 014		**NT**	A	*CR*	AL	58814		58847
165 015	*	**CR**	A	*CR*	AL	58815		58848
165 016		**NT**	A	*CR*	AL	58816		58849
165 017		**NT**	A	*CR*	AL	58817		58850
165 018	*	**CR**	A	*CR*	AL	58818		58851
165 019		**NT**	A	*CR*	AL	58819		58852
165 020		**NT**	A	*CR*	AL	58820		58853
165 021		**NT**	A	*CR*	AL	58821		58854
165 022		**NT**	A	*CR*	AL	58822		58855
165 023		**NT**	A	*CR*	AL	58873		58867
165 024	*	**CR**	A	*CR*	AL	58874		58868
165 025		**NT**	A	*CR*	AL	58875		58869
165 026	*	**CR**	A	*CR*	AL	58876		58870
165 027		**NT**	A	*CR*	AL	58877		58871
165 028		**NT**	A	*CR*	AL	58878		58872
165 029	*	**CR**	A	*CR*	AL	58823	55404	58856
165 030		**NT**	A	*CR*	AL	58824	55405	58857
165 031		**NT**	A	*CR*	AL	58825	55406	58858
165 032	*	**CR**	A	*CR*	AL	58826	55407	58859
165 033		**NT**	A	*CR*	AL	58827	55408	58860
165 034	*	**CR**	A	*CR*	AL	58828	55409	58861
165 035		**NT**	A	*CR*	AL	58829	55410	58862
165 036	*	**CR**	A	*CR*	AL	58830	55411	58863
165 037		**NT**	A	*CR*	AL	58831	55412	58864
165 038		**NT**	A	*CR*	AL	58832	55413	58865
165 039		**NT**	A	*CR*	AL	58833	55414	58866

CLASS 165/1   NETWORK TURBO   BREL

Thames Trains units. DMCL–MS–DMS or DMCL–DMS.

Construction: Welded aluminium.
Engines: One Perkins 2006-TWH of 260 kW (350 h.p.) at 1900 r.p.m.
Bogies: BREL P3-17 (powered), BREL T3-17 (non-powered).
Couplers: BSI.
Seating Layout: 1: 2+2 facing, 2: 3+2 facing/unidirectional.
Dimensions: 23.50 x 2.85 m.

Gangways: Within unit only.
Doors: Twin-leaf swing plug.
Wheel Arrangement: 2-B (– B-2) – B-2.
Maximum Speed: 90 m.p.h.
Multiple Working: Within class and with Classes 166 and 168.

58953–58969. DMCL. Lot No. 31098 BREL York 1992. 16/66 1T. 37.0 t.
58879–58898. DMCL. Lot No. 31096 BREL York 1992. 16/72 1T. 37.0 t.
MS. Lot No. 31099 BREL 1992. –/106. 37.0 t.
DMS. Lot No. 31097 BREL 1992. –/98. 37.0 t.

165 101	TT	A	TT	RG	58953	55415	58916
165 102	TT	A	TT	RG	58954	55416	58917
165 103	TT	A	TT	RG	58955	55417	58918
165 104	TT	A	TT	RG	58956	55418	58919
165 105	TT	A	TT	RG	58957	55419	58920
165 106	TT	A	TT	RG	58958	55420	58921
165 107	TT	A	TT	RG	58959	55421	58922
165 108	TT	A	TT	RG	58960	55422	58923
165 109	TT	A	TT	RG	58961	55423	58924
165 110	TT	A	TT	RG	58962	55424	58925
165 111	TT	A	TT	RG	58963	55425	58926
165 112	TT	A	TT	RG	58964	55426	58927
165 113	TT	A	TT	RG	58965	55427	58928
165 114	TT	A	TT	RG	58966	55428	58929
165 116	TT	A	TT	RG	58968	55430	58931
165 117	TT	A	TT	RG	58969	55431	58932
165 118	TT	A	TT	RG	58879	58933	
165 119	TT	A	TT	RG	58880	58934	
165 120	TT	A	TT	RG	58881	58935	
165 121	TT	A	TT	RG	58882	58936	
165 122	TT	A	TT	RG	58883	58937	
165 123	TT	A	TT	RG	58884	58938	
165 124	TT	A	TT	RG	58885	58939	
165 125	NT	A	TT	RG	58886	58940	
165 126	TT	A	TT	RG	58887	58941	
165 127	TT	A	TT	RG	58888	58942	
165 128	TT	A	TT	RG	58889	58943	
165 129	NT	A	TT	RG	58890	58944	
165 130	TT	A	TT	RG	58891	58945	
165 131	TT	A	TT	RG	58892	58946	
165 132	NT	A	TT	RG	58893	58947	
165 133	NT	A	TT	RG	58894	58948	
165 134	NT	A	TT	RG	58895	58949	
165 135	NT	A	TT	RG	58896	58950	
165 136	NT	A	TT	RG	58897	58951	
165 137	NT	A	TT	RG	58898	58952	

CLASS 166   NETWORK EXPRESS TURBO   ABB

DMCL(A)–MS–DMCL(B). Thames Trains units, built for Paddington–Oxford/
Newbury services.
Air conditioned.

Construction: Welded aluminium.
Engines: One Perkins 2006-TWH of 260 kW (350 h.p.) at 1900 r.p.m.
Bogies: BREL P3-17 (powered), BREL T3-17 (non-powered).
Couplers: BSI.
Seating Layout: 1: 2+2 facing, 2: 3+2 facing/unidirectional. 20 standard class seats in 2+2 format in DMCL(B).
Dimensions: 23.50 x 2.85 m.
Gangways: Within unit only.   **Wheel Arrangement:** 2-B – B-2 – B-2.
Doors: Twin-leaf swing plug.   **Maximum Speed:** 90 m.p.h.
Multiple Working: Within class and with Classes 165 and 168.

DMCL (A). Lot No. 31116 ABB York 1992–1993. 16/75 1T. 40.62 t.
MS. Lot No. 31117 ABB York 1992–1993. –/96. 38.04 t.
DMCL (B). Lot No. 31116 ABB York 1992–1993. 16/72 1T. 40.64 t.

166 201	TT	A	TT	RG	58101	58601	58122
166 202	TT	A	TT	RG	58102	58602	58123
166 203	TT	A	TT	RG	58103	58603	58124
166 204	TT	A	TT	RG	58104	58604	58125
166 205	TT	A	TT	RG	58105	58605	58126
166 206	TT	A	TT	RG	58106	58606	58127
166 207	TT	A	TT	RG	58107	58607	58128
166 208	TT	A	TT	RG	58108	58608	58129
166 209	TT	A	TT	RG	58109	58609	58130
166 210	TT	A	TT	RG	58110	58610	58131
166 211	TT	A	TT	RG	58111	58611	58132
166 212	TT	A	TT	RG	58112	58612	58133
166 213	TT	A	TT	RG	58113	58613	58134
166 214	TT	A	TT	RG	58114	58614	58135
166 215	TT	A	TT	RG	58115	58615	58136
166 216	TT	A	TT	RG	58116	58616	58137
166 217	TT	A	TT	RG	58117	58617	58138
166 218	TT	A	TT	RG	58118	58618	58139
166 219	TT	A	TT	RG	58119	58619	58140
166 220	TT	A	TT	RG	58120	58620	58141
166 221	TT	A	TT	RG	58121	58621	58142

CLASS 168 CLUBMAN ADTRANZ/BOMBARDIER

Various formations. Air conditioned.

Construction: Welded aluminium bodies with bolt-on steel ends.
Engines: One MTU 6R183TD13H of 315 kW (422 h.p.) at 1900 r.p.m.
Transmission: Hydraulic. Voith T211rzze to ZF final drive.
Bogies: One Adtranz P3–23 and one BREL T3–23 per car.
Couplers: BSI.
Seating Layout: 2+2 facing/unidirectional.
Dimensions: 23.62 x 2.69 m.
Gangways: Within unit only.   **Wheel Arrangement:** 2-B (– B-2 – B-2) – B-2.
Doors: Twin-leaf swing plug.   **Maximum Speed:** 100 m.p.h.
Multiple Working: Within class and with Classes 165 and 166.

Note: Fitted with tripcocks for working over London Underground tracks between Harrow-on-the-Hill and Amersham.

Class 168/0. Original Design. DMSL(A)–MSL–MS–DMSL(B).

58151–58155. DMSL(A). Adtranz Derby 1997–1998. –/60 1TD 1W. 43.7 t.
58651–58655. MSL. Adtranz Derby 1998. –/73 1T. 41.0 t.
58451–58455. MS. Adtranz Derby 1998. –/77. 40.5 t.
58251–58255. DMSL(B). Adtranz Derby 1998. –/68 1T. 43.6 t.

Note: 58451–58455 were formerly numbered 58656–58660 in 168 106–168 110.

168 001	**CR**	P	*CR*	AL	58151	58651	58451	58251
168 002	**CR**	P	*CR*	AL	58152	58652	58452	58252
168 003	**CR**	P	*CR*	AL	58153	58653	58453	58253
168 004	**CR**	P	*CR*	AL	58154	58654	58454	58254
168 005	**CR**	P	*CR*	AL	58155	58655	58455	58255

Class 168/1. These units are effectively Class 170s. DMSL(A)–(MS)–MSL–DMSL(B).

58156–58163. DMSL(A). Adtranz Derby 2000. –/59 1TD 2W. 43.7 t.
58756–58757. MSL. Bombardier Derby 2002. –/73 1T. 41.0 t.
58456–58460. MS. Bombardier Derby 2002. –/76. 40.5 t.
58461–58463. MS. Adtranz Derby 2000. –/76. 42.4 t.
58256–58263. DMSL(B). Adtranz Derby 2000. –/69 1T. 43.6 t.

Notes: 58461–58463 have been renumbered from 58661–58663.
58756 and 58757 have been renumbered from 58656 and 58657.

168 106	**CR**	P	*CR*	AL	58156	58456	58756	58256
168 107	**CR**	P	*CR*	AL	58157	58457	58757	58257
168 108	**CR**	P	*CR*	AL	58158	58458		58258
168 109	**CR**	P	*CR*	AL	58159	58459		58259
168 110	**CR**	P	*CR*	AL	58160	58460		58260
168 111	**CR**	H	*CR*	AL	58161	58461		58261
168 112	**CR**	H	*CR*	AL	58162	58462		58262
168 113	**CR**	H	*CR*	AL	58163	58463		58263

Class 168/2. These units are effectively Class 170s. Fitted with databus system. DMSL–(MS)–DMSL.

58164–58169. DMSL(A). Bombardier Derby 2003–2004. –/59 1TD 2W. 45.4 t.
58464/58468/58469. MS. Bombardier Derby 2003–2004. –/76. 44.0 t.
58264–58269. DMSL(B). Bombardier Derby 2003–2004. –/69 1T. 45.4 t.

168 214	**CR**	P	*CR*	AL	58164	58464	58264
168 215	**CR**	P	*CR*	AL	58165		58265
168 216	**CR**	P	*CR*	AL	58166		58266
168 217	**CR**	P	*CR*	AL	58167		58267
168 218	**CR**	P			58168	58468	58268
168 219	**CR**	P			58169	58469	58269

CLASS 170 TURBOSTAR ADTRANZ/BOMBARDIER

Various formations. Air conditioned.

Construction: Welded aluminium bodies with bolt-on steel ends.
Engines: One MTU 6R183TD13H of 315 kW (422 h.p.) at 1900 r.p.m.
Transmission: Hydraulic. Voith T211rzze to ZF final drive.
Bogies: One Adtranz P3–23 and one BREL T3–23 per car.
Couplers: BSI.
Seating Layout: 1: 2+1 facing/unidirectional (2+2 in first class in Class 170/1 end cars). 2: 2+2.
Dimensions: 23.62 x 2.69 m.
Gangways: Within unit only.   **Wheel Arrangement:** 2-B (– B-2) – B-2.
Doors: Twin-leaf swing plug.   **Maximum Speed:** 100 m.p.h.
Multiple Working: Within class and with Classes 150, 153, 155, 156, 158, 159.

Class 170/1. Midland Mainline units. DMCL–MCRMB–DMCL or DMCL–DMCL.

DMCL (A). Adtranz Derby 1998–1999. 12/45 1TD 2W. 45.19 t.
MCRMB. Adtranz Derby 2001. 24/24 and bar. 43.00 t.
DMCL (B). Adtranz Derby 1998–1999. 12/52 1T. Catering point. 45.22 t

Note: The DMCL(A) and DMCL(B) in the 3-car units have had their former first class end sections declassified.

170 101	**MM**	P	*MM*	DY	50101	55101	79101
170 102	**MM**	P	*MM*	DY	50102	55102	79102
170 103	**MM**	P	*MM*	DY	50103	55103	79103
170 104	**MM**	P	*MM*	DY	50104	55104	79104
170 105	**MM**	P	*MM*	DY	50105	55105	79105
170 106	**MM**	P	*MM*	DY	50106	55106	79106
170 107	**MM**	P	*MM*	DY	50107	55107	79107
170 108	**MM**	P	*MM*	DY	50108	55108	79108
170 109	**MM**	P	*MM*	DY	50109	55109	79109
170 110	**MM**	P	*MM*	DY	50110	55110	79110
170 111	**MM**	P	*MM*	DY	50111		79111
170 112	**MM**	P	*MM*	DY	50112		79112
170 113	**MM**	P	*MM*	DY	50113		79113
170 114	**MM**	P	*MM*	DY	50114		79114
170 115	**MM**	P	*MM*	DY	50115		79115
170 116	**MM**	P	*MM*	DY	50116		79116
170 117	**MM**	P	*MM*	DY	50117		79117

Class 170/2. Anglia Railways 3-car units. DMCL–MSLRB–DMSL.

DMCL. Adtranz Derby 1999. 29/3 1TD 2W. 44.30 t.
MSLRB. Adtranz Derby 1999. –/58 1T. Buffet and guard's office 42.76 t.
DMSL. Adtranz Derby 1999. –/66 1T. 44.70 t.

170 201	**AN**	P	*AR*	NC	50201	56201	79201
170 202	**AN**	P	*AR*	NC	50202	56202	79202
170 203	**AN**	P	*AR*	NC	50203	56203	79203
170 204	**AN**	P	*AR*	NC	50204	56204	79204
170 205	**AN**	P	*AR*	NC	50205	56205	79205

170 206	**AN**	P	*AR*	NC	50206	56206	79206
170 207	**AN**	P	*AR*	NC	50207	56207	79207
170 208	**AN**	P	*AR*	NC	50208	56208	79208

Class 170/2. Anglia Railways 2-car units. DMSL–DMCL.

DMSL. Bombardier Derby 2002. –/57 1TD 2W. 44.30 t.
DMCL. Bombardier Derby 2002. 9/53 1T. 44.70 t.

170 270	**AN**	P	*AR*	NC	50270	79270
170 271	**AN**	P	*AR*	NC	50271	79271
170 272	**AN**	P	*AR*	NC	50272	79272
170 273	**AN**	P	*AR*	NC	50273	79273

Class 170/3. South West Trains units. DMCL–DMCL.

50301–50308. DMCL(A). Adtranz Derby 2000. 9/43 1TD 2W. 45.80 t.
50392. DMCL(A). Bombardier Derby 2003. Fitted with databus system. 9/43 1TD 2W. . t.
79301–79308. DMCL(B). Adtranz Derby 2000. 9/53 1T. 45.80 t.
79392. DMCL(B). Bombardier Derby 2003. Fitted with databus system. 9/53 1T. . t.

Note: 170 392 was initially numbered 170 727 in error and painted into South Central livery before being repainted into South West Trains livery.

170 301	**SW**	P	*SW*	SA	50301	79301
170 302	**SW**	P	*SW*	SA	50302	79302
170 303	**SW**	P	*SW*	SA	50303	79303
170 304	**SW**	P	*SW*	SA	50304	79304
170 305	**SW**	P	*SW*	SA	50305	79305
170 306	**SW**	P	*SW*	SA	50306	79306
170 307	**SW**	P	*SW*	SA	50307	79307
170 308	**SW**	P	*SW*	SA	50308	79308
170 392	**SW**	P			50392	79392

Class 170/3. Hull Trains units. On order. DMCL–MSLRB–DMSL.

DMCL. Bombardier Derby 2004. 29/5 1TD 2W. 44.30 t.
MSLRB. Bombardier Derby 2004. –/60 1T. Buffet and guard's office 42.76 t.
DMSL. Bombardier Derby 2004. –/71 1T. 44.70 t.

170 393		P			50393	56393	79393
170 394		P			50394	56394	79394
170 395		P			50395	56395	79395
170 396		P			50396	56396	79396

Class 170/3. Porterbrook spot hire units. DMCL–MC–DMCL.

DMCL(A). Bombardier Derby 2002. 9/43 1TD 1W. 45.40 t.
MC. Bombardier Derby 2002. 22/36. 41.60 t.
DMCL(B). Bombardier Derby 2002. 9/53 1T. 45.80 t.

Advertising Livery:

170 397 "Q-Jump". Sky blue with purple doors.

| 170 397 | **AL** | P | *CT* | TS | 50397 | 56397 | 79397 |
| 170 398 | **P** | P | *CT* | TS | 50398 | 56398 | 79398 |

Class 170/3. Porterbrook spot hire unit. DMCL–DMCL.

DMCL(A). Bombardier Derby 2001. 9/43 1TD 2W. 45.40 t.
DMCL(B). Bombardier Derby 2001. 9/53 1T. 45.80 t.

Advertising Livery:

170 399 "Visit Birmingham" – European Capital of Culture 2008 (cerise pink with blue, orange, purple and green spots).

| 170 399 | **AL** | P | *CT* | TS | 50399 | | 79399 |

Class 170/4. ScotRail "express" units. DMCL–MS–DMCL.

DMCL(A). Adtranz Derby 1999–2001. 9/43 1TD 2W. 45.80 t.
MS. Adtranz Derby 1999–2001. –/76. 43.00 t.
DMCL(B). Adtranz Derby 1999–2001. 9/53 1T. 45.80 t.

170 401	**SR**	P	*SR*	HA	50401	56401	79401
170 402	**SR**	P	*SR*	HA	50402	56402	79402
170 403	**SR**	P	*SR*	HA	50403	56403	79403
170 404	**SR**	P	*SR*	HA	50404	56404	79404
170 405	**SR**	P	*SR*	HA	50405	56405	79405
170 406	**SR**	P	*SR*	HA	50406	56406	79406
170 407	**SR**	P	*SR*	HA	50407	56407	79407
170 408	**SR**	P	*SR*	HA	50408	56408	79408
170 409	**SR**	P	*SR*	HA	50409	56409	79409
170 410	**SR**	P	*SR*	HA	50410	56410	79410
170 411	**SR**	P	*SR*	HA	50411	56411	79411
170 412	**SR**	P	*SR*	HA	50412	56412	79412
170 413	**SR**	P	*SR*	HA	50413	56413	79413
170 414	**SR**	P	*SR*	HA	50414	56414	79414
170 415	**SR**	P	*SR*	HA	50415	56415	79415
170 416	**SR**	H	*SR*	HA	50416	56416	79416
170 417	**SR**	H	*SR*	HA	50417	56417	79417
170 418	**SR**	H	*SR*	HA	50418	56418	79418
170 419	**SR**	H	*SR*	HA	50419	56419	79419
170 420	**SR**	H	*SR*	HA	50420	56420	79420
170 421	**SR**	H	*SR*	HA	50421	56421	79421
170 422	**SR**	H	*SR*	HA	50422	56422	79422
170 423	**SR**	H	*SR*	HA	50423	56423	79423
170 424	**SR**	H	*SR*	HA	50424	56424	79424

Class 170/4. ScotRail "express" units. Fitted with databus system. DMCL–MS–DMSL or DMCL–MS–DMSL (see notes below).

DMCL. Bombardier Derby 2003–2004. 9/43 1TD 2W. 45.80 t.
MS. Bombardier Derby 2003–2004. –/76. 43.00 t.
DMSL. Bombardier Derby 2003–2004. –/67 1T. 45.80 t.

IMPORTANT NOTE: 170 425–170 432 are to be delivered DMCL–MS–DMSL, to become DMCL–MS–DMCL. The DMSL/DMCLs of units 170 425–170 432 and

170 450–170 457 will be swapped when the latter units have been delivered.

170 425	**SR**	P	*SR*	HA	50425	56425	79450
170 426	**SR**	P	*SR*	HA	50426	56426	79451
170 427	**SR**	P			50427	56427	79452
170 428	**SR**	P			50428	56428	79453
170 429	**SR**	P			50429	56429	79454
170 430	**SR**	P			50430	56430	79455
170 431	**SR**	P			50431	56431	79456
170 432	**SR**	P			50432	56432	79457
170 433	**SR**	P			50433	56433	79433
170 434	**SR**	P			50434	56434	79434

Class 170/4. ScotRail "suburban" units. On order. Fitted with databus system. DMSL–MS–DMCL or DMSL–MS–DMSL (see notes below).

DMSL. Bombardier Derby 2003–2004. –/55 1TD 2W. 45.80 t.
MS. Bombardier Derby 2003–2004. –/76. 43.00 t.
DMCL. Bombardier Derby 2003–2004. 9/53 1T. 45.80 t.

IMPORTANT NOTE: 170 450–170 457 to be delivered DMSL–MS–DMCL, to become DMSL–MS–DMSL. The DMCL/DMSLs of units 170 450–170 457 and 170 425–170 432 will be swapped when the suburban units have been delivered.

170 450	**SR**	P			50450	56450	79425
170 451	**SR**	P			50451	56451	79426
170 452	**SR**	P			50452	56452	79427
170 453	**SR**	P			50453	56453	79428
170 454	**SR**	P			50454	56454	79429
170 455	**SR**	P			50425	56455	79430
170 456	**SR**	P			50426	56456	79431
170 457	**SR**	P			50427	56457	79432
170 458	**SR**	P			50428	56458	79458
170 459	**SR**	P			50429	56459	79459
170 460	**SR**	P			50430	56460	79460
170 461	**SR**	P			50431	56461	79461

Class 170/4. ScotRail units. Standard class only units for Strathclyde PTE. 170 472–170 478 on order. DMSL–MS–DMSL.

50470–50471. DMSL(A). Adtranz Derby 2001. –/55 1TD 2W. 45.80 t.
50472–50478. DMSL(A). Bombardier Derby 2004–2005. Fitted with databus system. –/55 1TD 2W.   . t.
56470–56471. MS. Adtranz Derby 2001. –/76. 43.00 t.
56472–56478. MS. Bombardier Derby 2004–2005. Fitted with databus system. –/76.   . t.
79470–79471. DMSL(B). Adtranz Derby 2001. –/67 1T. 45.80 t.
79472–79478. DMSL(B). Bombardier Derby 2004–2005. Fitted with databus system. –/67 1T.   . t.

| 170 470 | **SP** | P | *SR* | HA | 50470 | 56470 | 79470 |
| 170 471 | **SP** | P | *SR* | HA | 50471 | 56471 | 79471 |

170 472	**SP**	P			50472	56472	79472
170 473	**SP**	P			50473	56473	79473
170 474	**SP**	P			50474	56474	79474
170 475	**SP**	P			50475	56475	79475
170 476	**SP**	P			50476	56476	79476
170 477	**SP**	P			50477	56477	79477
170 478	**SP**	P			50478	56478	79478

Class 170/5. Central Trains 2-car units. DMSL–DMSL.

DMSL(A). Adtranz Derby 1999–2000. –/55 1TD 2W. 45.80 t.
DMSL(B). Adtranz Derby 1999–2000. –/67 1T. 46.80 t.

Advertising Liveries:

170 505 – Bullring shopping centre, Birmingham – black and brown with various images.
170 513 – Robin Hood Line promotional livery – lime green, green and red with various images.

170 501	r	**CT**	P	CT	TS	50501	79501
170 502	r	**CT**	P	CT	TS	50502	79502
170 503	r	**CT**	P	CT	TS	50503	79503
170 504	r	**CT**	P	CT	TS	50504	79504
170 505	r	**AL**	P	CT	TS	50505	79505
170 506	r	**CT**	P	CT	TS	50506	79506
170 507	r	**CT**	P	CT	TS	50507	79507
170 508	r	**CT**	P	CT	TS	50508	79508
170 509	r	**CT**	P	CT	TS	50509	79509
170 510	r	**CT**	P	CT	TS	50510	79510
170 511	r	**CT**	P	CT	TS	50511	79511
170 512	r	**CT**	P	CT	TS	50512	79512
170 513	r	**AL**	P	CT	TS	50513	79513
170 514	r	**CT**	P	CT	TS	50514	79514
170 515	r	**CT**	P	CT	TS	50515	79515
170 516	r	**CT**	P	CT	TS	50516	79516
170 517	r	**CT**	P	CT	TS	50517	79517
170 518	r	**CT**	P	CT	TS	50518	79518
170 519	r	**CT**	P	CT	TS	50519	79519
170 520	r	**CT**	P	CT	TS	50520	79520
170 521	r	**CT**	P	CT	TS	50521	79521
170 522	r	**CT**	P	CT	TS	50522	79522
170 523	r	**CT**	P	CT	TS	50523	79523

Class 170/6. Central Trains 3-car units. DMSL–MS–DMSL.

DMSL(A). Adtranz Derby 2000. –/55 1TD 2W. 45.80 t.
MS. Adtranz Derby 2000. –/74. 43.00 t.
DMSL(B). Adtranz Derby 2000. –/67 1T. 46.80 t.

170 630	r	**CT**	P	CT	TS	50630	56630	79630
170 631	r	**CT**	P	CT	TS	50631	56631	79631
170 632	r	**CT**	P	CT	TS	50632	56632	79632
170 633	r	**CT**	P	CT	TS	50633	56633	79633
170 634	r	**CT**	P	CT	TS	50634	56634	79634

170 635	r	**CT**	P	*CT*	TS	50635	56635	79635
170 636	r	**CT**	P	*CT*	TS	50636	56636	79636
170 637	r	**CT**	P	*CT*	TS	50637	56637	79637
170 638	r	**CT**	P	*CT*	TS	50638	56638	79638
170 639	r	**CT**	P	*CT*	TS	50639	56639	79639

Class 170/7. South Central units. Fitted with databus system. 170 727–170 729 and 170 731–170 736 on order. DMCL–DMSL or DMCL–MS–MS–DMSL.

DMCL. Bombardier Derby 2003–2004. 9/43 1TD 2W. . t.
MS. Bombardier Derby 2003–2004. –/76. . t.
DMSL. Bombardier Derby 2003–2004. –/64 1T. . t.

170 721	**SN**	P	*SC*	SU	50721	79721		
170 722	**SN**	P	*SC*	SU	50722	79722		
170 723	**SN**	P	*SC*	SU	50723	79723		
170 724	**SN**	P	*SC*	SU	50724	79724		
170 725	**SN**	P	*SC*	SU	50725	79725		
170 726	**SN**	P	*SC*	SU	50726	79726		
170 727	**SN**	P			50727	79727		
170 728	**SN**	P			50728	79728		
170 729	**SN**	P			50729	79729		
170 731	**SN**	P			50731	56731	54731	79731
170 732	**SN**	P			50732	56732	54732	79732
170 733	**SN**	P			50733	56733	54733	79733
170 734	**SN**	P			50734	56734	54734	79734
170 735	**SN**	P			50735	56735	54735	79735
170 736	**SN**	P			50736	56736	54736	79736

171 802

CLASS 175   CORADIA 1000   ALSTOM

Air Conditioned.

Construction: Steel.
Engines: One Cummins N14 of 335 kW (450 h.p.).
Transmission: Hydraulic. Voith T211rzze to ZF final drive.
Bogies:
Couplers: Scharfenberg.
Seating Layout: 2+2 facing/unidirectional.
Dimensions: 23.71/23.03 x 2.73 m.
Gangways: Within unit only.   **Wheel Arrangement:** 2-B (– B-2) – B-2.
Doors: Single-leaf swing plug.   **Maximum Speed:** 100 m.p.h.
Multiple Working: Within class and with Class 180.

Note: Although operated by Wales & Borders, several Class 175s are hired back to First North Western for Manchester Airport to Blackpool North/Barrow & Millom/Windermere services.

Class 175/0. DMSL–DMSL. 2-car units.

DMSL(A). Alstom Birmingham 1999–2000. –/54 1TD 2W. 51.00 t.
DMSL(B). Alstom Birmingham 1999–2000. –/64 1T. 51.00 t.

175 001	FS	A	WB	CH	50701	79701
175 002	FS	A	WB	CH	50702	79702
175 003	FS	A	WB	CH	50703	79703
175 004	FS	A	WB	CH	50704	79704
175 005	FS	A	WB	CH	50705	79705
175 006	FS	A	WB	CH	50706	79706
175 007	FS	A	WB	CH	50707	79707
175 008	FS	A	WB	CH	50708	79708
175 009	FS	A	WB	CH	50709	79709
175 010	FS	A	WB	CH	50710	79710
175 011	FS	A	WB	CH	50711	79711

Names (carried on one side of each DMSL):

175 004	MENCAP National Colleges Pengwern College
175 006	Brondyffryn Trust
175 008	Valhalla Blackpool Pleasure Beach

Class 175/1. DMSL–MSL–DMSL. 3-car units.

DMSL(A). Alstom Birmingham 1999–2001. –/54 1TD 2W. 51.00 t.
MSL. Alstom Birmingham 1999–2001. –/68 1T. 43 t 68 1T. 47.50 t.
DMSL(B). Alstom Birmingham 1999–2001. –/64 1T. 51.00 t.

175 101	FS	A	WB	CH	50751	56751	79751
175 102	FS	A	WB	CH	50752	56752	79752
175 103	FS	A	WB	CH	50753	56753	79753
175 104	FS	A	WB	CH	50754	56754	79754
175 105	FS	A	WB	CH	50755	56755	79755
175 106	FS	A	WB	CH	50756	56756	79756
175 107	FS	A	WB	CH	50757	56757	79757
175 108	FS	A	WB	CH	50758	56758	79758
175 109	FS	A	WB	CH	50759	56759	79759
175 110	FS	A	WB	CH	50760	56760	79760
175 111	FS	A	WB	CH	50761	56761	79761
175 112	FS	A	WB	CH	50762	56762	79762
175 113	FS	A	WB	CH	50763	56763	79763
175 114	FS	A	WB	CH	50764	56764	79764
175 115	FS	A	WB	CH	50765	56765	79765
175 116	FS	A	WB	CH	50766	56766	79766

Names (carried on one side of each DMSL):

175 103	Mum
175 107	CORONATION ST. ROVERS RETURN
175 111	Brief Encounter
175 112	South Lakes Wild Animal Park SUMATRAN TIGER
175 114	Commonwealth Cruiser
175 116	PETER VL JONES

CLASS 180   CORADIA 1000   ALSTOM

Air Conditioned.

Construction: Steel.
Engines: One Cummins QSK19 of 560 kW (750 h.p.) at 2100 r.p.m.
Transmission: Hydraulic. Voith T312br to Voith final drive.
Bogies: Alstom MB2.
Couplers: Scharfenberg.
Seating Layout: 1: 2+1 facing/unidirectional, 2: 2+2 facing/unidirectional.
Dimensions: 23.71/23.03 x 2.73 m.
Gangways: Within unit only.
Wheel Arrangement: 2-B – B-2 – B-2 – B–2 – B-2.
Doors: Single-leaf swing plug.   **Maximum Speed:** 125 m.p.h.
Multiple Working: Within class and with Class 175.

DMSL(A). Alstom Birmingham 2000–2001. –/46 2W 1TD. 53.00 t.
MFL. Alstom Birmingham 2000–2001. 42/– 1T 1W + catering point. 51.50 t.
MSL. Alstom Birmingham 2000–2001. –/68 1T. 51.50 t.
MSLRB. Alstom Birmingham 2000–2001. –/56 1T. 51.50 t.
DMSL(B). Alstom Birmingham 2000–2001. –/56 1T. 53.00 t.

180 101	FG	A	GW	OM	50901	54901	55901	56901	59901
180 102	FG	A	GW	OM	50902	54902	55902	56902	59902
180 103	FG	A	GW	OM	50903	54903	55903	56903	59903
180 104	FG	A	GW	OM	50904	54904	55904	56904	59904
180 105	FG	A	GW	OM	50905	54905	55905	56905	59905
180 106	FG	A	GW	OM	50906	54906	55906	56906	59906
180 107	FG	A	GW	OM	50907	54907	55907	56907	59907
180 108	FG	A	GW	OM	50908	54908	55908	56908	59908
180 109	FG	A	GW	OM	50909	54909	55909	56909	59909
180 110	FG	A	GW	OM	50910	54910	55910	56910	59910
180 111	FG	A	GW	OM	50911	54911	55911	56911	59911
180 112	FG	A	GW	OM	50912	54912	55912	56912	59912
180 113	FG	A	GW	OM	50913	54913	55913	56913	59913
180 114	FG	A	GW	OM	50914	54914	55914	56914	59914

2. DIESEL ELECTRIC UNITS

The following features are standard to ex-BR Southern Region diesel-electric multiple unit power cars (Classes 201–207):

Construction: Steel.
Engine: One English Electric 4SRKT Mk. 2 of 450 kW (600 h.p.) at 850 r.p.m.
Main Generator: English Electric EE824.
Traction Motors: Two English Electric EE507 mounted on the inner bogie.

Bogies: SR Mk. 4. (Former EMU TSL vehicles have Commonwealth bogies).
Couplers: Drophead buckeye.
Doors: Manually operated slam.
Brakes: Electro-pneumatic and automatic air.
Maximum Speed: 75 m.p.h.
Multiple Working: Other ex BR Southern Region DEMU vehicles.

CLASS 201/202 PRESERVED 'HASTINGS' UNIT BR

DMBS–2TSL–TSRB–TSL–DMBS.

Preserved unit made up from 2 Class 201 short-frame cars and 2 Class 202 long-frame cars. The 'Hastings' units were made with narrow body-profiles for use on the section between Tonbridge and Battle which had tunnels of restricted loading gauge. These tunnels were converted to single track operation in the 1980s thus allowing standard loading gauge stock to be used. The set also contains a Class 411 EMU trailer (not Hastings line gauge).

Gangways: Within unit only.
Seating Layout: 2+2 facing.
Dimensions: 18.36 x 2.50 m (60000/60501), 20.34 x 2.50 m. (60118/60529) 20.34 x 2.82 m (69337/70262).

60000. DMBS. Lot No. 30329 Eastleigh 1957. –/22. 54 t.
60501. TSL. Lot No. 30331 Eastleigh 1957. –/52 2T. 29 t.
70262. TSL (ex Class 411/5 EMU). Lot No. 30455 Eastleigh 1958–1959. –/64 2T. 33.78 t.
69337. TSRB (ex Class 422 EMU). Lot No. 30805 York 1970. –/40. 35 t.
60529. TSL. Lot No. 30397 Eastleigh 1957. –/60 2T. 30 t.
60118. DMBS. Lot No. 30395 Eastleigh 1957. –/30. 55 t.

201 001	**G**	HD *SS*	SE	60000 60529 70262 69337 60501 60118

Names:

60000	Hastings		60118	Tunbridge Wells

CLASS 205/0 (3H)   BR 'HAMPSHIRE'

DMBS–TSL–DTCsoL or DMBS–DTCsoL.

Gangways: Non-gangwayed.
Seating Layout: 3+2 facing or compartments.
Dimensions: 20.33 x 2.82 m (DMBS), 20.28 x 2.82 m (TS), 20.36 x 2.82 m (DTCsoL).

60111/60117/60154. DMBS. Lot No. 30332 Eastleigh 1957. –/52. 56 t.
60122/60124. DMBS. Lot No. 30540 Eastleigh 1958–1959. –/52. 56 t.
60146–60151. DMBS. Lot No. 30671 Eastleigh 1960–1962. –/42. 56 t.
60650/60658. TS. Lot No. 30542 Eastleigh 1958–1959. –/104. 30 t.
60673–60678. TS. Lot No. 30672 Eastleigh 1960–1962. –/104. 30 t.
60800–60808. DTCsoL. Lot No. 30333 Eastleigh 1956–1957. 13/50 2T. 32 t.
60811. DTCsoL. Lot No. 30333 Eastleigh 1956–1957. 19/50 2T. 32 t.
60820. DTCsoL. Lot No. 30399 Eastleigh 1957–1958. 13/50 2T. 32 t.
60824. DTCsoL. Lot No. 30541 Eastleigh 1958–1959. 13/50 2T. 32 t.
60827–60832. DTCsoL. Lot No. 30673 Eastleigh 1960–1962. 13/62 2T. (13/60 2T 60827, 13/57 2T 60831, 32 t.

205 001	**CX**	P	*SC*	SU	60154		60800
205 009	**CX**	P	*SC*	SU	60108	60658	60808
205 012	**CX**	P	*SC*	SU	60111		60811
205 018	**CX**	P	*SC*	SU	60117	60674	60828
205 025	**CX**	P	*SC*	SU	60124		60824
205 028	**CX**	P	*SC*	SU	60146	60673	60827
205 032	**CX**	P	*SC*	SU	60150	60677	60831
205 033	**CX**	P	*SC*	SU	60151	60678	60832

CLASS 205/2 (3H)   BR 'HAMPSHIRE'

DMBS–DTSL. Refurbished 1980. Fluorescent lighting. PA.

Details as for Class 205/0 except:

Gangways: Within unit only.
Seating Layout: 3+2 facing.

DMBS. Lot No. 30332 Eastleigh 1957. –/39. 57 t.
DTSL. Lot No. 30333 Eastleigh 1957. –/76 2T. 32 t.

| 205 205 | **CX** | P | *SC* | SU | 60110 | | 60810 |

CLASS 207/0 (2D)   BR 'OXTED'

DMBS–DTS (formerly DMBS–TCsoL–DTS).

This class was built for the Oxted line and therefore referred to as 'Oxted' units. They were made with a narrower body-profile which also allowed them to be used through the restricted loading-gauge Somerhill Tunnel between Tonbridge and Grove Junction (Tunbridge Wells). This tunnel was converted to single track operation in the 1980s thus allowing standard loading gauge stock to be used.

Gangways: Non-gangwayed.
Seating Layout: 2+2 facing.
Dimensions: 20.33 x 2.74 m (DMBS/TCsoL), 20.32 x 2.74 m. (DTS).

DMBS. Lot No. 30625 Eastleigh 1962. –/42. 56 t.
DTS. Lot No. 30627 Eastleigh 1962. –/76. 32 t.

207 017	**CX**	P	*SC*	SU	60142	60916

CLASS 207/2 (3D)   BR 'OXTED'

Refurbished Class 207 units. DMBS–TSL–DTS.
Gangwayed sets with an ex-Class 411 EMU trailer in the centre.

Gangways: Within unit only.
Seating Layout: 2+2 facing.
Dimensions: 20.34 x 2.74 m (DMBS), 20.32 x 2.74 m. (DTS).

DMBS. Lot No. 30625 Eastleigh 1962. –/40. 56 t.
70547/70549. TSL. Lot No. 30620 Eastleigh 1960–1961 –/64 2T. 33.78 t.
DTS. Lot No. 30627 Eastleigh 1962. –/73. 32 t.

207 202	**CX**	P	*SC*	SU	60130	70549	60904
207 203	**CX**	P	*SC*	SU	60127	70547	60901

Name (carried on DMBS):

207 202 Brighton Royal Pavilion

CLASS 220   VOYAGER   BOMBARDIER

DMS–MS–MSRMB–DMF.

Construction: Steel.
Engine: Cummins of 750 h.p. (560 kW) at 1800 r.p.m.
Transmission: Two Alstom Onix 800 three-phase traction motors of 275 kW.
Braking: Rheostatic and electro-pneumatic.
Bogies: Bombardier B5005.
Couplers: Dellner.
Seating Layout: 1: 2+1 facing/unidirectional, 2: 2+2 mainly unidirectional.
Dimensions: 23.85/22.82 x 2.73 m.
Gangways: Within unit only.
Wheel Arrangement: 1A-A1 – 1A-A1 – 1A-A1 – 1A-A1.
Doors: Single-leaf swing plug.
Maximum Speed: 125 m.p.h.
Multiple Working: Within class and with Classes 221 and 222.

DMS. Bombardier Brugge/Wakefield 2000–2001. –/42 1TD 1W. 48.10 t.
MS. Bombardier Brugge/Wakefield 2000–2001. –/62 1TD 1W. 45.00 t.
MSRMB. Bombardier Brugge/Wakefield 2000–2001. –/58. 48.00 t.
DMF. Bombardier Brugge/Wakefield 2000–2001. 26/– 1TD 1W. 44.50 t.

220 001	VT	HX	VX	CZ	60301	60701	60201	60401
220 002	VT	HX	VX	CZ	60302	60702	60202	60402
220 003	VT	HX	VX	CZ	60303	60703	60203	60403
220 004	VT	HX	VX	CZ	60304	60704	60204	60404
220 005	VT	HX	VX	CZ	60305	60705	60205	60405
220 006	VT	HX	VX	CZ	60306	60706	60206	60406
220 007	VT	HX	VX	CZ	60307	60707	60207	60407
220 008	VT	HX	VX	CZ	60308	60708	60208	60408
220 009	VT	HX	VX	CZ	60309	60709	60209	60409
220 010	VT	HX	VX	CZ	60310	60710	60210	60410
220 011	VT	HX	VX	CZ	60311	60711	60211	60411
220 012	VT	HX	VX	CZ	60312	60712	60212	60412
220 013	VT	HX	VX	CZ	60313	60713	60213	60413
220 014	VT	HX	VX	CZ	60314	60714	60214	60414
220 015	VT	HX	VX	CZ	60315	60715	60215	60415
220 016	VT	HX	VX	CZ	60316	60716	60216	60416
220 017	VT	HX	VX	CZ	60317	60717	60217	60417
220 018	VT	HX	VX	CZ	60318	60718	60218	60418
220 019	VT	HX	VX	CZ	60319	60719	60219	60419
220 020	VT	HX	VX	CZ	60320	60720	60220	60420
220 021	VT	HX	VX	CZ	60321	60721	60221	60421
220 022	VT	HX	VX	CZ	60322	60722	60222	60422
220 023	VT	HX	VX	CZ	60323	60723	60223	60423
220 024	VT	HX	VX	CZ	60324	60724	60224	60424
220 025	VT	HX	VX	CZ	60325	60725	60225	60425
220 026	VT	HX	VX	CZ	60326	60726	60226	60426
220 027	VT	HX	VX	CZ	60327	60727	60227	60427
220 028	VT	HX	VX	CZ	60328	60728	60228	60428

220 029	**VT**	HX	*VX*	CZ	60329	60729	60229	60429
220 030	**VT**	HX	*VX*	CZ	60330	60730	60230	60430
220 031	**VT**	HX	*VX*	CZ	60331	60731	60231	60431
220 032	**VT**	HX	*VX*	CZ	60332	60732	60232	60432
220 033	**VT**	HX	*VX*	CZ	60333	60733	60233	60433
220 034	**VT**	HX	*VX*	CZ	60334	60734	60234	60434

Names (carried on MS):

220 001	Somerset Voyager	220 019	Mersey Voyager
220 002	Forth Voyager	220 020	Wessex Voyager
220 003	Solent Voyager	220 021	Staffordshire Voyager
220 004	Cumbrian Voyager	220 022	Brighton Voyager
220 005	Guildford Voyager	220 023	Mancunian Voyager
220 006	Clyde Voyager	220 024	Sheffield Voyager
220 007	Thames Voyager	220 025	Severn Voyager
220 008	Draig Gymreig/Welsh Dragon	220 026	Stagecoach Voyager
220 009	Gatwick Voyager	220 027	Avon Voyager
220 010	Ribble Voyager	220 028	Black Country Voyager
220 011	Tyne Voyager	220 029	Vyajer Kernewek/
220 012	Lanarkshire Voyager		Cornish Voyager
220 013	Gwibiwr De Cymru/South	220 030	Devon Voyager
	Wales Voyager	220 031	Tay Voyager
220 014	South Yorkshire Voyager	220 032	Grampian Voyager
220 015	Solway Voyager	220 033	Fife Voyager
220 016	Midland Voyager	220 034	Yorkshire Voyager
220 017	BOMBARDIER Voyager		
220 018	Dorset Voyager		

▲ Refurbished and reliveried Chiltern Railways unit 165 036 is seen at Quainton Road with a special Bank Holiday service to Aylesbury on 26/05/03. **Mervyn Turvey**

▼ Thames Trains-liveried 166 209 approaches Didcot with a London Paddington–Oxford train on 18/07/03. **Jonathan Allen**

▲ New Chiltern 3-car unit 168 214 stands at Dorridge having arrived with a special working in connection with the reopening of Birmingham Moor Street Station concourse on 11/10/03. **Alan Yearsley**

▼ South West Trains-liveried 170 303 is seen forming the 16.06 Romsey–Totton (via Chandlers Ford) service on 09/07/03, at St. Denys. **Mervyn Turvey**

▲ Strathclyde PTE-liveried 170 470 passes Larbert with the 10.19 Stirling–Glasgow Queen Street on 04/07/03.   **Ian Lothian**

▼ First Group (suburban)-liveried 175 008 is seen at Burneside with the 17.46 Oxenholme–Windermere "shuttle" on 16/08/02. All Class 175s are now operated by Wales & Borders, but some are hired back to First North Western.   **Ian Lothian**

180 114 is seen at Coedkernew with First Great Western's 10.30 Swansea–London Paddington on 21/07/03.

Bob Sweet

▲ The last services for the Class 205 "Thumper" DEMUs will be the through Uckfield–London "commuter" services. On 13/06/03 205 028 and 205 001 race through Clapham Junction with the 07.27 Uckfield–London Victoria. **Brian Denton**

▼ Still in Connex livery, from the days of Connex South Central, 207 017 pauses at Crowborough on 02/08/03 with an Uckfield–Oxted "shuttle" service. **Alan Barnes**

Virgin Voyager 220 006 heads west past Flax Bourton as it leaves Bristol with the
07.51 Newcastle–Plymouth on 14/07/03.   **John Chalcraft**

▲ 221 121 passes Wilmorton, Derby on 03/09/03 with the 08.50 Plymouth–Edinburgh (diverted via Leicester). **Paul Robertson**

▼ Railtrack-liveried departmental test unit 977693/694 (converted from a Class 101) is seen at Carlisle on 13/06/03. **Robert Pritchard**

▲ Railtrack-liveried track assessment unit 999600/601 (based on a Class 150) is seen at Colton Junction on 16/07/02 with the 09.00 Inverness–Derby.
Paul Robertson

▼ EurorailScout GB-liveried track assessment/recording unit 999700/701 passes Winwick on 23/01/03 with a Carnforth–Derby test run. **Alan Sherratt**

CLASS 221   SUPER VOYAGER   BOMBARDIER

DMS–MSRMB–MS(–MS)–DMF. Tilting units.

Construction: Steel.
Engine: Cummins of 750 h.p. (560 kW) at 1800 r.p.m.
Transmission: Two Alstom Onix 800 three-phase traction motors of 275 kW.
Braking: Rheostatic and electro-pneumatic.
Bogies: Bombardier HVP.
Couplers: Dellner.
Seating Layout: 1: 2+1 facing/unidirectional, 2: 2+2 mainly unidirectional.
Dimensions: 23.85/22.82 x 2.73 m.
Gangways: Within unit only.
Wheel Arrangement: 1A-A1 – 1A-A1 – 1A-A1 (– 1A-A1) – 1A-A1.
Doors: Single-leaf swing plug.
Maximum Speed: 125 m.p.h.
Multiple Working: Within class and with Classes 220 and 222.

DMS. Bombardier Brugge/Wakefield 2001–2002. –/42 1TD 1W. 58.30 t.
MSRMB. Bombardier Brugge/Wakefield 2001–2002. –/58. 58.00 t.
MS. Bombardier Brugge/Wakefield 2001–2002. –/62 1TD 1W. 55.80 t.
DMF. Bombardier Brugge/Wakefield 2001–2002. 26/– 1TD 1W. 54.90 t.

221 101	VT	HX	VX	CZ	60351	60751	60951	60851	60451
221 102	VT	HX	VX	CZ	60352	60752	60952	60852	60452
221 103	VT	HX	VX	CZ	60353	60753	60953	60853	60453
221 104	VT	HX	VX	CZ	60354	60754	60954	60854	60454
221 105	VT	HX	VX	CZ	60355	60755	60955	60855	60455
221 106	VT	HX	VX	CZ	60356	60756	60956	60856	60456
221 107	VT	HX	VX	CZ	60357	60757	60957	60857	60457
221 108	VT	HX	VX	CZ	60358	60758	60958	60858	60458
221 109	VT	HX	VX	CZ	60359	60759	60959	60859	60459
221 110	VT	HX	VX	CZ	60360	60760	60960	60860	60460
221 111	VT	HX	VX	CZ	60361	60761	60961	60861	60461
221 112	VT	HX	VX	CZ	60362	60762	60962	60862	60462
221 113	VT	HX	VX	CZ	60363	60763	60963	60863	60463
221 114	VT	HX	VX	CZ	60364	60764	60964	60864	60464
221 115	VT	HX	VX	CZ	60365	60765	60965	60865	60465
221 116	VT	HX	VX	CZ	60366	60766	60966	60866	60466
221 117	VT	HX	VX	CZ	60367	60767	60967	60867	60467
221 118	VT	HX	VX	CZ	60368	60768	60968	60868	60468
221 119	VT	HX	VX	CZ	60369	60769	60969	60869	60469
221 120	VT	HX	VX	CZ	60370	60770	60970	60870	60470
221 121	VT	HX	VX	CZ	60371	60771	60971	60871	60471
221 122	VT	HX	VX	CZ	60372	60772	60972	60872	60472
221 123	VT	HX	VX	CZ	60373	60773	60973	60873	60473
221 124	VT	HX	VX	CZ	60374	60774	60974	60874	60474
221 125	VT	HX	VX	CZ	60375	60775	60975	60875	60475
221 126	VT	HX	VX	CZ	60376	60776	60976	60876	60476
221 127	VT	HX	VX	CZ	60377	60777	60977	60877	60477
221 128	VT	HX	VX	CZ	60378	60778	60978	60878	60478

	VT	HX	VX	CZ					
221 129	VT	HX	*VX*	CZ	60379	60779	60979	60879	60479
221 130	VT	HX	*VX*	CZ	60380	60780	60980	60880	60480
221 131	VT	HX	*VX*	CZ	60381	60781	60981	60881	60481
221 132	VT	HX	*VX*	CZ	60382	60782	60982	60882	60482
221 133	VT	HX	*VX*	CZ	60383	60783	60983	60883	60483
221 134	VT	HX	*VX*	CZ	60384	60784	60984	60884	60484
221 135	VT	HX	*VX*	CZ	60385	60785	60985	60885	60485
221 136	VT	HX	*VX*	CZ	60386	60786	60986	60886	60486
221 137	VT	HX	*VX*	CZ	60387	60787	60987	60887	60487
221 138	VT	HX	*VX*	CZ	60388	60788	60988	60888	60488
221 139	VT	HX	*VX*	CZ	60389	60789	60989	60889	60489
221 140	VT	HX	VX	CZ	60390	60790	60990	60890	60490
221 141	VT	HX	*VX*	CZ	60391	60791	60991		60491
221 142	VT	HX	*VX*	CZ	60392	60792	60992		60492
221 143	VT	HX	*VX*	CZ	60393	60793	60993		60493
221 144	VT	HX	*VX*	CZ	60394	60794	60994		60494

Names (carried on MS No. 609xx):

221 101	Louis Bleriot		221 123	Henry Hudson
221 102	John Cabot		221 124	Charles Lindbergh
221 103	Christopher Columbus		221 125	Henry the Navigator
221 104	Sir John Franklin		221 126	Captain Robert Scott
221 105	William Baffin		221 127	Wright Brothers
221 106	Willem Barents		221 128	Captain John Smith
221 107	Sir Martin Frobisher		221 129	George Vancouver
221 108	Sir Ernest Shackleton		221 130	Michael Palin
221 109	Marco Polo		221 131	Edgar Evans
221 110	James Cook		221 132	William Speirs Bruce
221 111	Roald Amundsen		221 133	Alexander Selkirk
221 112	Ferdinand Magellan		221 134	Mary Kingsley
221 113	Sir Walter Raleigh		221 135	Donald Campbell
221 114	Sir Francis Drake		221 136	Yuri Gagarin
221 115	Sir Francis Chichester		221 137	Mayflower Pilgrims
221 116	David Livingstone		221 138	Thor Heyerdahl
221 117	Sir Henry Morton Stanley		221 139	Leif Erikson
221 118	Mungo Park		221 140	Vasco da Gama
221 119	Amelia Earhart		221 141	Amerigo Vespucci
221 120	Amy Johnson		221 142	Matthew Flinders
221 121	Charles Darwin		221 143	Auguste Picard
221 122	Doctor Who		221 144	Prince Madoc

CLASS 222   MERIDIAN   BOMBARDIER

Various formations. New 4-car and 9-car units on order for Midland Mainline.

Construction: Steel.
Engine: Cummins of 750 h.p. (560 kW) at 1800 r.p.m.
Transmission: Two Alstom Onix 800 three-phase traction motors of 275 kW.
Braking: Rheostatic and electro-pneumatic.
Bogies: Bombardier B5005.

Couplers: Dellner.
Seating Layout: 1: 2+1, 2: 2+2 facing/unidirectional.
Dimensions: 23.85/22.82 x 2.73 m.
Gangways: Within unit only.
Wheel Arrangement: All cars 1A-A1.
Doors: Single-leaf swing plug.
Maximum Speed: 125 m.p.h.
Multiple Working: Within class and with Classes 220 and 221.

DMRFO. Bombardier Brugge/Wakefield 2002–2004. 22/– 1TD 1W.   . t.
MFO. Bombardier Brugge/Wakefield 2002–2004. 42/– 1T.   . t.
MCO. Bombardier Brugge/Wakefield 2002–2004. 28/20 1T.   . t.
MSORMB. Bombardier Brugge/Wakefield 2002–2004. –/62.   . t.
MSO. Bombardier Brugge/Wakefield 2002–2004. –/70 1T.   . t.
DMSO. Bombardier Brugge/Wakefield 2002–2004. –/36 1TD 2W.   . t.

222 001–222 007. DMRFO–MFO–MFO–MSO–MSO–MSORMB–MSO–MSO–DMSO. 9-car units.

222 001	**MN**	H	60161	60531	60541	60551	60561
			60621	60341	60441	60241	
222 002	**MN**	H	60162	60532	60542	60552	60562
			60622	60342	60442	60242	
222 003	**MN**	H	60163	60533	60543	60553	60563
			60623	60343	60443	60243	
222 004	**MN**	H	60164	60534	60544	60554	60564
			60624	60344	60444	60244	
222 005	**MN**	H	60165	60535	60545	60555	60565
			60625	60345	60445	60245	
222 006	**MN**	H	60166	60536	60546	60556	60566
			60626	60346	60446	60246	
222 007	**MN**	H	60167	60537	60547	60557	60567
			60627	60347	60447	60247	

222 008–222 023. DMRFO–MSO–MSORMB–DMSO. 4-car units.

222 008	**MN**	H	60168	60628	60918	60248
222 009	**MN**	H	60169	60629	60919	60249
222 010	**MN**	H	60170	60630	60920	60250
222 011	**MN**	H	60171	60631	60921	60251
222 012	**MN**	H	60172	60632	60922	60252
222 013	**MN**	H	60173	60633	60923	60253
222 014	**MN**	H	60174	60634	60924	60254
222 015	**MN**	H	60175	60635	60925	60255
222 016	**MN**	H	60176	60636	60926	60256
222 017	**MN**	H	60177	60637	60927	60257
222 018	**MN**	H	60178	60638	60928	60258
222 019	**MN**	H	60179	60639	60929	60259
222 020	**MN**	H	60180	60640	60930	60260
222 021	**MN**	H	60181	60641	60931	60261
222 022	**MN**	H	60182	60642	60932	60262
222 023	**MN**	H	60183	60643	60933	60263

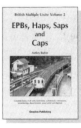

3. SERVICE DMUS

This section lists vehicles not used for passenger-carrying purposes. Some vehicles are numbered in the special service stock number series.

CLASS 114/1   ROUTE LEARNING UNIT

DMB–DT. Converted 1992 from Class 114/1. Gangwayed within unit.

Construction: Steel.
Engines: Two Leyland TL11/40 of 153 kW (205 h.p.) at 1950 r.p.m.
Transmission: Mechanical. Cardan shaft and freewheel to a four-speed epicyclic gearbox with a further cardan shaft to the final drive, each engine driving the inner axle of one bogie.

Maximum Speed: 70 m.p.h.	**Couplings:** Screw.
Bogies: DD9 + DT9.	**Multiple Working:** Blue Square.
Brakes: Twin pipe vacuum.	**Dimensions:** 20.45 x 2.82 m.

Non-Standard Livery: Grey, red and yellow.

977775. DMB. Lot No. 30209 Derby 1957. 38.0 t.
977776. DT. Lot No. 30210 Derby 1957. 30.0 t.

-     **0**   E   TE   977775   (55928)   <u>977776   (54904)</u>

CLASS 122   ROUTE LEARNING UNIT

DM. Converted 1995 from DMBS. Non gangwayed single car with cab at each end.

Construction: Steel.
Engines: Two Leyland 1595 of 112 kW (150 h.p.) at 1800 r.p.m.
Transmission: Mechanical. Cardan shaft and freewheel to a four-speed epicyclic gearbox with a further cardan shaft to the final drive, each engine driving the inner axle of one bogie.

Maximum Speed: 75 m.p.h.	**Couplings:** Screw.
Bogies: DD10.	**Multiple Working:** Blue Square.
Brakes: Twin pipe vacuum.	**Dimensions:** 20.45 x 2.82 m.

Doors: Manually operated slam.

55012. DM. Lot No. 30419 Gloucester 1958. Converted by ABB Doncaster 1995. 36.5 t.

-     **LH**   E   TE   55012

CLASS 930   SANDITE/DE-ICING UNIT

DMB–T–DMB. Converted 1993 from Class 205. Gangwayed within unit. Sandite trailer 977870 is replaced by de-icing trailer 977364 as required.

Construction: Steel.
Engine: One English Electric 4SRKT Mk. 2 of 450 kW (600 h.p.) at 850 r.p.m.
Transmission: Electric. Two English Electric EE507 traction motors mounted on the bogie at the non-driving end of each power car.
Maximum Speed: 75 m.p.h.   **Bogies:** SR Mk. 4.
Brakes: Electro-pneumatic and automatic air.
Doors: Manually operated slam.   **Couplings:** Drophead buckeye.
Multiple Working: Classes 201–207.
Dimensions: 20.33 x 2.82 x 3.87 m. (DMB); 20.28 x 2.82 m.

977939–977940. DMB. Lot No. 30671 Eastleigh 1962. 56.0 t.
977870. T. Lot No. 30542 Eastleigh 1960. 30.5 t.

930 301	**RO**	NR	*SC*	SU	977939	(60145)	977870	(60660)
					977940	(60149)		

CLASS 960 ULTRASONIC TESTING/TRACTOR UNIT

DM–DM. Converted 1986 from Class 101. Gangwayed within unit. Often operates with either 975091 or 999602 as a centre car.

For detail see page 10 except:

Brakes: Air.

977391. DM. Lot No. 30500 Metro-Cammell. 1959. 32.5 t.
977392. DM. Lot No. 30254 Metro-Cammell. 1956. 32.5 t.

-	**RK**	NR	*SO*	RG	977391	(51433)	977392	(53167)

CLASS 960   TEST UNIT (Iris 2)

DM–DM. Converted 1991 from Class 101. Gangwayed within unit.

For details see page 10.

977693. DM. Lot No. 30261 Metro-Cammell. 1957. 32.5 t.
977694. DM. Lot No. 30276 Metro-Cammell. 1958. 32.5 t.

-	**RK**	NR	*SO*	BY	977693	(53222)	977694	(53338)

CLASS 960　　　　　　　SANDITE & SERVICE UNITS

DMB. Converted 1991/1993 from Class 121. Non gangwayed.

For details see page 11.

977723. DMB. Lot No. 30518 Pressed Steel 1960. 38.0 t.
977858–60/66/73. DMB. Lot No. 30518 Pressed Steel 1960. 38.0 t.

960 010	M	NR	CR	AL	977858	(55024)
960 011	RK	NR	BB	AP	977859	(55025)
960 012	N	NR		AP	977860	(55028)
960 013	N	NR		AL	977866	(55030)
960 014	N	NR		AL	977873	(55022)
960 021	RO	NR	CR	AL	977723	(55021)

CLASS 960　　　　　　　　EMERGENCY TRAIN UNITS

Under conversion from Class 121 for Severn Tunnel emergency train.
For details see page 11.

DMB. Lot No. 30518 Pressed Steel 1960. 38.5 t.

960 0	RK	NR	CP	977975	(55027)
960 0	RK	NR	CP	977976	(55031)

CLASS 960　　　　　　　　TRACK ASSESSMENT UNIT

Converted from Class 121. **For details see page 11.**

977968. DMB.

977968	ES	ES	CA	RU	55029

CLASS 960　　　　　　　　　　　　SANDITE UNIT

DMB. Converted 1991 from Class 122. Non gangwayed.

Construction: Steel.
Engines: Two Leyland 1595 of 112 kW (150 h.p.) at 1800 r.p.m.
Transmission: Mechanical. Cardan shaft and freewheel to a four-speed epicyclic gearbox with a further cardan shaft to the final drive, each engine driving the inner axle of one bogie.
Maximum Speed: 70 m.p.h.
Bogies: DD10.　　　　　　　　　　**Couplings:** Screw.
Brakes: Twin pipe vacuum.　　　　**Multiple Working:** Blue Square.
Doors: Manually operated slam.　　**Dimensions:** 20.45 x 2.82 m.

975042. DMB. Lot No. 30419 Gloucester 1958. 36.5 t.

960 015	RO	NR	CR	AL	975042	(55019)

CLASS 960   SANDITE UNIT

DMB. Converted 2003 from Class 117. Non gangwayed.

Construction: Steel.
Engines: Two Leyland 1595 of 112 kW (150 h.p.) at 1800 r.p.m.
Transmission: Mechanical. Cardan shaft and freewheel to a four-speed epicyclic gearbox with a further cardan shaft to the final drive, each engine driving the inner axle of one bogie.
Maximum Speed: 70 m.p.h.
Bogies: DD10.   **Couplings:** Screw.
Brakes: Twin pipe vacuum.   **Multiple Working:** Blue Square.
Doors: Manually operated slam.   **Dimensions:** 20.45 x 2.82 m.

977987/977988. DMB. Lot No. 30419 Gloucester 1958. 36.5 t.

960 301   **G**   CR *CR*   AL   977987 (51371)   977988 (51413)

UNCLASSIFIED   DE-ICING UNIT

T. Converted 1960 from 4-Sub EMU vehicle. Non gangwayed. Operates with 977939/40.

Construction: Steel.
Maximum Speed: 70 m.p.h.   **Couplings:** Drophead buckeye.
Bogies: Central 43 inch.   **Multiple Working:** SR system.
Brakes: Electro-pneumatic and automatic air.
Doors: Manually operated slam.   **Dimensions:**

977364. T. Southern Railway Eastleigh 1946. 29.0 t.

-          **RO**   NR *SC*   SU   977364   (10400)

CLASS 960   TRACK ASSESSMENT UNIT

DM–DM. Purpose built service unit. Gangwayed within unit.

Construction: Steel.
Engine: One Cummins NT-855-RT5 of 213 kW (285 h.p.) at 2100 r.p.m. per power car.
Transmission: Hydraulic. Voith T211r with cardan shafts to Gmeinder GM190 final drive.
Maximum Speed: 75 m.p.h.   **Couplers:** BSI automatic.
Bogies: BP38 (powered), BT38 (non-powered).
Brakes: Electro-pneumatic.   **Dimensions:** 20.06 x 2.82 m.
Doors: Manually operated slam & power operated sliding.
Multiple Working: Classes 142, 143, 144, 150, 153, 155, 156, 158, 159, 170.

999600. DM. Lot No. 4060 BREL York 1987. 36.5 t.
999601. DM. Lot No. 4061 BREL York 1987. 36.5 t.

-         **RK**   NR *SO*   ZA   999600 999601

CLASS 960   ULTRASONIC TEST UNIT

T. Converted 1986 from Class 432 EMU. Gangwayed. Operates with 977391/2.

Construction: Steel.
Bogies: SR Mk. 6.
Brakes: Twin pipe vacuum.
Doors: Manually operated slam.

Maximum Speed: 70 m.p.h.
Couplings: Screw.
Multiple Working: Blue Square.
Dimensions: 19.66 x 2.82 m.

999602. T. Lot No. 30862 York 1974. 55.5 t.

| - | RK | NR | *SO* | ZA | 999602 | (62483) |

CLASS 960 TRACK ASSESSMENT/RECORDING UNIT

DM–DM. Universal track recording unit for video inspections, for measuring rail profiles etc. Plasser type UFM 160-1. Full details awaited.

Construction:
Transmission:
Maximum Speed: 100 m.p.h.
Brakes:

Engine:

Weight: 70 t.
Dimensions: 20.06 x 2.82 m.

999700. DM.
999701. DM.

| - | **ES** | ES | *CA* | RU | 999700 999701 |

CLASS 960 TRACK ASSESSMENT/RECORDING UNIT

DM. On order. Full details awaited.

Construction:
Transmission:
Maximum Speed: 100 m.p.h.
Brakes:

Engine:

Weight: 70 t.
Dimensions: 20.06 x 2.82 m.

DM.

| - | **ES** | ES | *CA* | RU | 999800 |

4. DMUS AWAITING DISPOSAL

The list below comprises vehicles awaiting disposal which are stored on the
Network Rail network, together with vehicles stored at other locations which,
although awaiting disposal, remain Network Rail registered.

Class 101

Note: All vehicles are classed as "spare" because all sets have in practise
been split at their respective storage locations.

Spare	**RR**	A	PY	51189	51429	51432	51496	51498	51506
				54055	54061	54347	54352	54365	54393
				54408					
Spare	**S**	A	PY	51187	51188	51231	51247	51435	51500
				51512	53268				
Spare	**BG**	A	PY	54350					
Spare	**RR**	A	LO	51175	51177	51230	51533	53211	53269
				54056	54085	54091			
Spare	**S**	A	LO	51253	53171				
Spare	**N**	A	LO	53311	53322				
Spare	**RR**	A	ZH	51224	51428	53163			
Spare	**S**	A	ZH	51185					
Spare	**BG**	A	NL	54342					
Spare	**RR**	A	BP	59303					
Spare	**G**	A	BP	59539					

Class 117

Note: All vehicles are classed as "spare" because all sets have in practise
been split at their respective storage locations.

Spare	**RR**	A	PY	51353	51381	51395	59486	59492	59500
				59509	59521				
Spare	**N**	A	PY	51335	51341	51350	51356	51358	51366
				51377	51383	51392	51398	51408	
Spare	**RR**	CR	AL	51411					

Class 141

141 106	**WY**	CD	ZF	55506	55526
141 112	**WY**	CD	ZF	55512	55532

Class 165

Spare	**NT**	A	ZC	58930

Class 205

Spare	**N**	AM	ZG	60650

Class 951

Spare	**N**	NR	ZG	977696

5. CODES

5.1. LIVERY CODES

Code	Description
AL	Advertising livery (see class heading for details).
AN	Anglia Railways Class 170s (white & turquoise with blue vignette).
AR	Anglia Railways (turquoise blue with a white stripe).
AV	Arriva Trains (white with white doors (with the addition of a cream "swish" on the Class 142s)).
BG	BR blue & grey lined out in white.
BI	"Visit Bristol" promotional livery (deep blue with various images).
CO	Centro (grey/green with light blue, white & yellow stripes).
CR	Chiltern Railways (blue & white with a thin red stripe).
CT	Central Trains (two-tone green with yellow doors. Blue flash and red strpe at vehicle ends.).
CX	Connex (white with yellow lower body & blue solebar).
DC	Scenic lines of Devon & Cornwall promotional livery (black with gold cantrail stripe).
ES	Eurailscout GB (Light orange with a blue and purple logo).
FG	First Group corporate Inter-City livery (indigo blue with a white roof & gold, pink & white stripes).
FS	First Group corporate regional/suburban livery (indigo blue with pink & white stripes).
G	BR Southern Region/SR or BR DMU green.
GP	Ginsters Cornish Pasties promotional livery (Black & red with various images and cartoons etc.)
HW	Heart of Wales Line promotional livery (orange with yellow doors).
LH	BR Loadhaul (black with orange cabsides).
M	BR maroon (Maroon lined out in straw & black).
MM	Old Midland Mainline (Teal green with cream lower body sides & three orange stripes).
MN	New Midland Mainline (Thin tangerine stripe on the lower bodyside, ocean blue, grey & white).
MT	Old Merseytravel (yellow/white with grey & black stripes).
MY	New Merseytravel (yellow/white with grey stripe).
N	BR Network SouthEast (white & blue with red lower bodyside stripe, grey solebar & cab ends).
NS	Northern Spirit/Arriva Trains Northern (turquoise blue with lime green 'N').
NT	BR Network SouthEast (white & blue with red lower bodyside & cantrail stripes).
NW	North West Trains/First North Western (blue with gold cantrail stripe & star).
O	Non standard livery (see class heading for details).
P	Porterbrook Leasing Company (purple & grey or white).
PS	Provincial Services (dark blue/grey with light blue & white stripes).
RE	Provincial Services/Regional Railways Express (light grey/buff/dark grey with white, dark blue & light blue stripes).

RK	New Railtrack (green & blue).
RN	North West Regional Railways (dark blue/grey with green & white stripes).
RO	Old Railtrack (orange with white & grey stripes).
RR	Regional Railways (dark blue/grey with light blue & white stripes, three narrow dark blue stripes at vehicle ends).
S	Old Strathclyde PTE (orange & black lined out in white).
SC	New Strathclyde PTE (carmine & cream lined out in black & gold).
SL	Silverlink (indigo blue with white stripe, green lower body & yellow doors).
SN	South Central (white & dark green with light green patch near cab ends).
SP	New Strathclyde PTE Class 170/334 livery (carmine & cream, with a turquoise stripe).
SR	ScotRail (white, terracotta, purple & aquamarine).
SW	South West Trains {long-distance stock} (white & dark blue with black window surrounds, red doors & red panel with orange stripe at unit ends).
TT	Thames Trains (blue with lime green doors).
TW	Tyne & Wear PTE (white & yellow with blue stripe).
TX	Arriva Trans-Pennine Express (plum with yellow 'N').
VL	Valley Lines (dark green & red with white & light green stripes. Light green doors).
VT	New Virgin Trains (silver, with black window surrounds, white cantrail stripe & red roof. Red swept down at unit ends. Black and white striped doors).
VW	Visit Wales promotional livery (green & red with various images).
WB	Wales & Borders Alphaline (metallic silver with blue doors).
WX	Heart of Wessex Line promotional livery (red with yellow doors).
WT	Wessex Trains Alphaline (metallic silver with maroon doors).
WY	Old West Yorkshire PTE (red/cream with thin yellow stripe).
WZ	Wessex Trains claret promotional livery with various images.
YN	West Yorkshire PTE (red with light grey 'N').
YP	New West Yorkshire PTE (red with grey semi-circles).

5.2. OWNER CODES

A	Angel Train Contracts
BC	Bridgend County Borough Council
CD	Cotswold Rail Ltd.
CR	Chiltern Railways
E	English Welsh & Scottish Railway
ES	Eurailscout GB
H	HSBC Rail (UK) Ltd.
HD	Hastings Diesels Ltd.
HX	Halifax Asset Finance Ltd.
NR	Network Rail
P	Porterbrook Leasing Company
RD	Rhondda Cynon Taff District Council
RI	Rail Assets Investments Ltd.

5.3. OPERATOR CODES

AR	Anglia Railways
AN	Arriva Trains Northern
AW	Arriva Trains Wales (to be formed from Wales & Borders)
BB	Balfour Beatty Rail
CA	Carillion Rail
CR	Chiltern Railways
CT	Central Trains
GW	First Great Western
MM	Midland Mainline
NR	Network Rail
NW	First North Western
SC	South Central
SL	Silverlink
SO	Serco Railtest
SR	ScotRail
SS	Normally used only on special or charter services
SW	South West Trains
TT	Thames Trains
VX	Virgin Cross-Country
VL	Wales & Borders Trains (Valley lines business unit)
WB	Wales & Borders Trains
WX	Wessex Trains

5.4. ALLOCATION & LOCATION CODES

Code	Location	Operator
AL	Aylesbury	Chiltern Railways
AP*	Ashford Rail Plant	Balfour Beatty Rail Plant
BP	Blackpool North sidings	*Storage location only*
BY	Bletchley	Silverlink
CF	Cardiff Canton	Wales & Borders/EWS
CH	Chester	Wales & Borders
CK	Corkerhill (Glasgow)	ScotRail
CP	Crewe Carriage	London & North Western Railway
CZ	Central Rivers (Burton)	Bombardier Transportation
DY	Derby Etches Park	Maintrain
HA	Haymarket (Edinburgh)	ScotRail
HT	Heaton (Newcastle)	Arriva Trains Northern
IS	Inverness	ScotRail
LO	Longsight Diesel (Manchester)	First North Western
NC	Norwich Crown Point	Anglia Railways
NH	Newton Heath (Manchester)	First North Western
NL	Neville Hill (Leeds)	Arriva Trains Northern/Maintrain
OM	Old Oak Common carriage(London)	First Great Western/Riviera Trains
PY	MoD DERA Shoeburyness	Ministry of Defence
RG	Reading	Thames Trains
RU*	Rugby Rail Plant	Carillion Rail Plant
SA	Salisbury	South West Trains
SE	St. Leonards (Hastings)	St. Leonards Railway Engineering
SU	Selhurst (Croydon)	South Central
TE	Thornaby	EWS
TS	Tyseley (Birmingham)	Maintrain
ZA	RTC Business Park (Derby)	Serco/AEA Technology
ZB	Doncaster Works	Wabtec
ZC	Crewe Works	Bombardier Transportation
ZD	Derby Litchurch Lane Works	Bombardier Transportation
ZF	Doncaster Works	Bombardier Transportation
ZG	Eastleigh Works	Alstom
ZH	Springburn Works Glasgow	Alstom
ZI	Ilford Works	Bombardier Transportation
ZK	Kilmarnock Works	Hunslet Barclay
ZN	Wolverton Works	Alstom
ZP	Horbury (Wakefield)	Bombardier Transportation

* = unofficial code.

ABBREVIATIONS

DERA   Defence Evaluation & Research Agency